EARLY JAPAN

GREAT AGES OF MAN

A History of the World's Cultures

EARLY JAPAN

by

JONATHAN NORTON LEONARD

and

The Editors of TIME-LIFE BOOKS

TIME-LIFE INTERNATIONAL (Nederland) B.V.

THE AUTHOR: Jonathan Norton Leonard is a staff writer for TIME-LIFE BOOKS. For 20 years he worked for TIME Magazine as Latin American and Science editor. In the latter position, Mr. Leonard handled stories that originated in every quarter of the globe, involving personalities of all nations. Although he has always been interested in Japan and the Japanese, his comprehension of the culture and accomplishments of that land has been greatly enriched with his development of this volume in collaboration with its consultants. Among Mr. Leonard's recently published books are *Ancient America,* in this Great Ages of Man Series, *Flight into Space, Exploring Science* and the volume *Planets* in the LIFE Science Library.

THE CONSULTING EDITOR: Leonard Krieger, Professor of History at Columbia University, was formerly Professor of History at Yale. Dr. Krieger is the author of *The German Idea of Freedom* and *The Politics of Discretion* and co-author of *History,* written in collaboration with John Higham and Felix Gilbert.

THE COVER: A samurai on horseback, clad in full battle regalia, storms after his foe during one of the civil wars that ravaged Japan in the 12th century.

CONTENTS

NOTE: THE PRESENT LOCATIONS OF ALL WORKS OF ART REPRODUCED IN THIS BOOK, AND THE NAMES OF THEIR CREATORS, ARE LISTED ON PAGE 187.

PREFACE

From earliest times, Japan has seemed to most Westerners a remote country inhabited by a strange people. Even in today's shrinking world the enigma, to a considerable extent, remains: a country with a strong martial tradition and yet skilled in the arts of peace, in production and in trade; an oriental State industrially based on an advanced Western technology; a people at once imitative and highly inventive; a maritime country whose inhabitants identify almost religiously with their land.

The pattern of Japan's unusual cultural history was set at an early stage. Geographically isolated from the great civilizations, it was not until the sixth century A.D. that Japan encountered, and enthusiastically embraced, Chinese culture and the Buddhist religion. Even so, despite the relatively primitive state of Japan's social and political organization, a great deal of the cultural absorption took the form of the adaptation to Japanese needs and interests of Chinese institutions and ideas. Nowhere was this more apparent than in the field of religion where, in the religious ceremonies associated with the Emperor's divinity, Buddhist and the native traditional Shinto elements became intermingled. At the same time, in the country as a whole, the more primitive Shinto religion survived alongside the imported Buddhist forms. Thus was displayed early that essentially Japanese capacity to live and believe on different planes and at different levels of sophistication. And when, because of internal troubles in China, Japan again became isolated in the ninth century A.D. she continued to develop the brilliant culture of the Heian period, which, despite its

admixture of Chinese elements, could still be called truly Japanese. Similarly in the more modern period, after the early encounters with the West and the diligent adoption of Western techniques, Japan withdrew, on this occasion deliberately, and during the time known as that of the Closed Country developed in her own distinctive way.

If the essential feature of art is the ordering of experience, then the Japanese people must rank high amongst the artistic peoples of the world. Animist in their traditional religion, they saw poetry and meaning in Nature in her violent as well as in her calmer moods; and if, in the remarkably beautiful Japanese countryside, it seems that Nature imitates Art, it is also true that often, as in the famous sand gardens of the Zen Buddhist temples and in flower arrangement, Art imitates Nature. It is the unitary and pervading nature of the Japanese aesthetic that is its most striking characteristic: the economy and the functional beauty of the most simple household objects; the poetry of violence and the sword in Bushido—the Way of the Warrior; the elaborate modes of social behaviour; the contemplative and ascetic disciplines of Zen Buddhism; the formalized homage to beauty in the tea ceremony.

Against the background of shifting political power and changing class relationships, through periods of stability and times of near-anarchy, Mr. Leonard shows us a country growing materially richer and, in its semi-isolation, using its wealth to enrich its cultural achievement. In a brilliant and evocative narrative he describes the development and flowering of that culture.

L. E. BARAGWANATH
Fellow of St. Catherine's College
University of Oxford

YELLOW SEA

SEA OF JAPAN

KOREA

STRAIGHTS OF KOREA

TSUSHIMA

IKI

HIRADO

HAKATA

HIROSHIMA

NAGASAKI

INLAND SEA

HEIAN-KYO (KYOTO)

LAKE BIWA

HIMEJI

OSAKA

NARA

NAGOYA

KYUSHU

SHIKOKU

SAKAI

ISE

EAST CHINA SEA

KAGOSHIMA

TANEGASHIMA

SEA OF OKHOTSK

HOKKAIDO

PACIFIC OCEAN

HONSHU

MT. FUJI

EDO (TOKYO)

KAMAKURA

VIEW OF
EARLY
JAPAN

700-1700

1

COUNTRY OF CONTRADICTIONS

A DISTINCTIVE SWORD GUARD *is an example of the Japanese aesthetic: a necessary item (a shield to protect the swordsman's hand) has been made beautiful. The blade passes through the centre of the crab design.*

Off the east coast of Asia, too far to be seen on the clearest day, lies the strange and wonderful Land of the Rising Sun—Japan. It is a curving chain of volcanic islands larger in area than Great Britain, smaller than France. On its four main islands of Kyushu, Shikoku, Honshu and Hokkaido, most of the land is mountainous. But among the peaks and forested crags are several fertile plains of considerable size, many flat-bottomed river valleys and innumerable smaller patches of arable soil. It is a beautiful land, and its temperate climate and dependable rainfall make it a delightful place for men to live.

But Japan is also a violent land. It lies squarely in the path of hurricanes, and nearly every year at least one great typhoon roars across its coasts, battering waterfronts, uprooting trees and filling narrow valleys with foaming floods. Another kind of violence comes from underground: active volcanoes belch fire and smoke, and earthquakes shake the islands from end to end.

The extraordinary beauty of Japan and the grim catastrophes that afflict it seem to have reflected themselves in the Japanese character—a contradictory and often startling mixture of delicacy and belligerence. Since ancient times the Japanese have ranked among the world's most ferocious warriors, but no other people has given more elaborate attention to courteous conduct or more loving devotion to flowers, poetry and art.

In a more direct way Japan's geography has affected its national culture. The Straights of Korea, which separate the westernmost island, Kyushu, from the nearest part of the Asiatic mainland, is 100 miles wide, and although it has sizeable stepping-stone islands, it was difficult and dangerous to cross in early times. These barrier straits gave Japan a semi-isolation, placing it within the Chinese cultural area and at the same time setting it apart. During certain periods a broad stream of knowledge, literature, art and religion flowed from China to Japan. At other times the flow was shut off from one side or the other, and Japan developed on its own. But whether in isolation or not, Japan was always itself. Everything that came from China, from household arts to philosophy, was reshaped to suit Japanese tastes and needs.

HOLLOW-EYED FIGURES, *depicting the faces of a girl, a man and a monkey, were among the thousands of cylindrical clay statues set in the ground around the burial mounds of early Japanese emperors, both as ornamentation and to stabilize the loose earth.*

Japan's past—from prehistory through the classical centuries of Japanese civilization—is especially fascinating because of the light it casts on modern Japan, many of whose distinctive and contrasting characteristics can be traced far back into antiquity. The emperor, for instance, is treated in much the same way today as he was 15 centuries ago. Although he is an important symbol of national unity and honoured as supreme ruler, he wields little temporal power. Almost equally ancient is the Japanese trait of eagerly courting foreign ideas for long periods, then suddenly turning indifferent or hostile to them—changing attitudes towards the outside world that have alternated repeatedly since very early times. The contrast between passionate artistry and the grimmest kind of combativeness is another ancient fixture in the life of the highly emotional Japanese. Sometimes one trait has been dominant, sometimes the other, but always both have existed. During the country's blood-drenched early feudal period, at the same time as the swords of fierce 12th-century samurai warriors were lopping off heads wholesale, the Japanese were also creating beautifully landscaped gardens, even as they do today. Still earlier, as powerful provincial warrior chieftains threatened the authority of tenth-century emperors, the blending of perfume was a complex and highly sophisticated

art and a courtier's ability to turn a poetic phrase was often a key to his success.

By 500 B.C., a millennium after the great land of China had achieved a high civilization, the chain of Japanese islands off its coast were still inhabited by rude tribesmen. Archaeological evidence indicates that some of them had been there for thousands of years, but who they were and where they came from is largely a mystery. It seems likely that they bore little racial resemblance to the Japanese, who are predominantly a Mongoloid people. Another ancient tribal group were the Ainu, a Stone Age folk who lived chiefly by hunting and fishing, worshipped bears and were notably hairy, which most Japanese are not. Some anthropologists think that the Ainu—a few of whom still live on the northern island of Hokkaido—were primitive members of the white race, a strain that split off from ancestral Caucasian stock in very ancient times. They may have arrived in Japan from Siberia and been fairly widespread until forced northwards by a more advanced people already established further south. These established inhabitants were not Mongoloid either, at any rate not in the clear sense that the Chinese are, and may have reached Japan from an undetermined homeland in northern Asia. They may have spoken a language similar in some ways to modern Japanese, which is wholly different from Chinese and may be distantly related to Korean.

During the second and first centuries B.C. truly Mongoloid immigrants or invaders crossed the Korea straits in considerable numbers, bringing with them all-important knowledge: how to grow rice in flooded paddies, how to weave coarse cloth and how to smelt iron and forge it into crude tools and weapons. They mixed with the earlier inhabitants and gradually adopted some of their customs and language. Like most early farmers, the people resulting from this amalgamation undoubtedly practised a form of nature-worship, deifying such phenomena as the sun and the moon, or an especially awesome mountain or waterfall.

This mixed culture, which was flourishing by the beginning of the Christian era, is known as Yayoi, from the site where archaeologists first excavated its remains. Glimpses of it also come from supercilious Chinese travellers, one of whom reported in A.D. 238 that south-western Japan, which he called Wa, was divided into many small States that were often ruled by sorceresses. Among these magic-working queens was a lady named Pimiko, who lived shut up in a fortified palace with 1,000 female attendants and one man to help her to communicate with her subjects. This ancient custom of rule by women was to continue intermittently in Japan until late in the eighth century. In fact, through much of Japan's early history women seem to have exercised considerable political and social influence, becoming completely subservient to men only after the 15th century. According to another Chinese account, "the people of Wa live on raw vegetables and go about barefooted. They smear their bodies with pink and scarlet. They serve food on bamboo and wooden trays, helping themselves with their fingers. When-

ever they undertake an enterprise or a journey and discussion arises, they bake bones and divine in order to tell whether fortune will be good or bad. When men of importance worship, they merely clap their hands instead of bowing or kneeling. If the lowly meet important men on the road, they stop and withdraw to the roadside. In addressing them, they either squat or kneel, with both hands on the ground to show respect. The people of Wa are very fond of strong drink".

About A.D. 250 this island country of mild barbarians governed by sorceress queens fell under sterner influences. Across the Korea straits came fierce Mongoloid horsemen, an invasion that was probably part of the explosion of Asian peoples destined to fling the Huns against the Roman Empire a century later. Little is known about them except that they fought in iron armour and wielded superior iron weapons. They may have been comparatively few in number, but their horsemanship and weapons, and perhaps their organization and fighting spirit, were responsible for bringing a new structure to Japanese society.

Soon the warlike horsemen became established as the aristocracy of Japan, and it was not many generations before one of their noble families, perhaps in alliance with native priest-aristocrats, won precedence over the others. By a miracle of continuity, this same Imperial Family, originating deep in the shadows of prehistory, still reigns over modern Japan.

Japanese mythology is richly embroidered with details about the divine origin of the Imperial Family. According to one myth, the first earthly member of the family was the grandson of Amaterasu, the sun-goddess. Sent down from heaven to establish order and bearing three precious symbols—the curved jewel, the sword and the mirror that even today are imperial tokens—"the august grandchild" landed in south-eastern Kyushu. One of his human descendants was Jimmu Tenno, the half-legendary first emperor of Japan, who enlarged his domain until it included the fertile Yamato plain on Honshu, near the modern city of Osaka. There he set up his capital and reigned for "more then 100 years".

Among these decorative mythological fancies runs a thread of fact. Archaeological and historical studies show that the Japanese State expanded from Kyushu and reached the Yamato region before A.D. 400. About this time the myths became fairly plausible records, giving the names of flesh-and-blood emperors and describing the bloody struggles for power among the armed factions that surrounded their Court.

Even then the emperor was already cast in the paradoxical role he was to fill through most of Japan's history—venerated as supreme, yet for all practical purposes more a religious symbol than a head of government. The real ruler was an official something like a prime minister. This powerful position was a prize fought for by various clans, who could muster armies of their own. There was no firm rule of succession; when an emperor died or was deposed, the great minister often decided which prince of the Imperial Family was to be his heir. Sometimes he had several young princes assassinated in order to head off future rivalries.

The first clan to win continuing control of the Court was the Soga family, which consolidated its power by marrying its daughters into the imperial line. Thus, upon the death of a ruler, the successor who ascended the throne always numbered the Soga among his closest relatives. Even when the new ruler was not a child, the strong family ties of Japan forced him to obey the orders of his Soga advisers. After a number of emperors had married Sogas, these ties became still stronger.

Emperors might be dethroned or murdered, but the royal family was never displaced, because its religious significance was too important. Only an authentic emperor, directly descended from the sun-goddess, could be held divine and could intercede with heaven on behalf of men. This ritual usefulness was to protect and preserve the Imperial Family through more than 1,500 years of vicissitudes.

Despite such intricate statecraft at the Yamato Court, Japan under the Soga was still a barbarous land. Its political organization had not progressed much beyond a loosely knit assemblage of clans tolerating the supremacy of one of their members, and its technology was far behind that of China or even Korea. There was no written language, and among its scattering of scholars only a few knew how to read or write Chinese. Communication was so poor that the central government had little influence over the turbulent clans beyond the Yamato region. Much of the country was frontier, plagued by outlaws and pirates or by unsubdued Ainu. But a great change was coming. Suddenly Japan became aware of the charms and advantages of Chinese civilization and eagerly welcomed everything Chinese.

The beginning of this period of marked Chinese influence is often given as A.D. 552, a year when China was emerging from centuries of disruptive wars and political chaos and was approaching one of the most illustrious epochs of its long history. It was beginning to mould itself into a great nation, wonderfully orderly by Japanese standards, and bursting with new religious, artistic and literary vigour. The more the Japanese learned about this dynamic country on the mainland, the more desirous they were to catch up with Chinese culture.

The year A.D. 552 stands out as a significant date in Japan's open-armed reception of mainland civilization, because it was in that year that the ruler of the Korean kingdom of Paikche, which had close cultural ties with China, appealed for Japanese help against his enemies. Along with his emissaries, he sent to the Yamato Court a bronze image of the Buddha, some Buddhist scriptures and a letter praising Buddhism, which had spread to Korea from its far-distant home in India and was now well established in China. Japan must have had earlier contacts with Buddhism, which was already 1,000 years old, but the king of Paikche's letter seems to have triggered a new burst of interest in this religion, and the powerful Soga family became its active partisans.

Iname, the high-ranking Soga minister at that time, appears to have viewed Buddhism not only as a handy carrier of Chinese culture and ideas but also as a political tool, and by favouring its acceptance he hoped to offset the power of native priest-politicians. He was also strongly attracted to Chinese theories of government that emphasized a central bureaucracy in the hands of powerful ministers. The Soga statesmen already dominated the Japanese Imperial Court. If the Chinese system could be set up, it would give them tight control of the outlying provinces as well.

Iname's politico-religious strategy threw Japan into 50 years of struggle between the advocates of Buddhism, which stressed ethical and spiritual virtue, and those clans wishing to retain the native religion, by now known as Shinto. The pressure for Buddhism and Chinese cultural ideas was maintained by Iname's son and successor Umako, who imported Chinese books and scholars, sent embassies and students to China and encouraged the founding of Buddhist monasteries. In these efforts he was supported by the man he selected in A.D. 593 as heir apparent, Crown Prince Shotoku.

Prince Shotoku is remembered as an idealized sage-ruler of the Chinese type, but he was probably more a symbol of Chinese culture than an active innovator in governmental matters; he accomplished few tangible reforms. The best-known work attributed to him is a document sometimes hailed as the first constitution of Japan. It is mostly Chinese-based moral preachments about the way the officials should behave, and it shows that Chinese influence was flooding into the country. Chinese customs and etiquette were becoming the fashion, and Japanese scholars were learning the difficult Chinese written language.

The death of Prince Shotoku in A.D. 622 was followed by a particularly bloody interval of civil warfare, during which the Soga clan was driven from power by a league of envious rivals and many of its members slaughtered. In A.D. 645 the Emperor Kotoku came to the throne under the tutelage of another clan, who came to be called Fujiwara and who were destined to be predominant for the next 500 years. The Soga policy of welcoming things Chinese, however, did not change, for by this time Chinese culture was more appealing.

The great mainland empire, now ruled by the T'ang Dynasty, had become the strongest, most advanced and civilized nation on earth. Between the seventh and early tenth centuries, while Europe was enduring the Dark Ages, its armies marched to the Caspian Sea; its traders and diplomats were in touch with India, Persia, even with Byzantium. Its capital, Ch'ang-an, was already the world's biggest city, with over a million people; from this fountain-head of culture, Chinese influences continued to flow into Japan in an ever-increasing stream.

One of the most important of these influences was Chinese religion. After initial opposition from defenders of Shinto, Chinese religious ideas, notably Chinese versions of Buddhism, became immensely popular, at least with the upper classes. Buddhism had changed a great deal since its supposed foundation by the Indian Prince Gautama, who lived in the sixth century B.C. Built on the Hindu concept of a never-ending cycle of reincarnation, the original Buddhist doctrines held that all life involves suffering and that death brings no relief because a new life begins after a previous life has ended. The only possible escape from this eternal repetition of suffering is "enlightenment", an awareness of the illusory nature of all existence, attainable only after the renunciation of desire through arduous study, discipline and meditation.

This mystical doctrine might not have appealed to seventh-century Japanese brought up in the unsophisticated, nature-orientated Shinto, but Buddhism had long since split, as Christianity later did, into innumerable sects with little resemblance to the original teaching of Prince Gautama. Some sects developed in China emphasized ethics and morality. Others incorporated belief in gods and heaven, and still others practised magical ritual or meditation. From these many varieties of Buddhism the Japanese selected and imported just those values and features that best suited their tastes.

What the Japanese apparently wanted of Buddhism in the early centuries of its introduction was a more efficacious and impressive way of interceding with the divine powers to ensure good crops and to ward off plagues and other disasters. Plenty of Buddhist sects were ready to fill this want, as well as more philosophical needs. Their priests came to Japan from Korea or China equipped with wonderfully colourful and moving rituals, brilliant vestments, chants, incantations, gongs, drums and incense. They brought Chinese-language sutras (holy scriptures) that had marvellous effects when read or recited. They imported beautiful images of the serene Buddha, as well as architects to build temples, and sculptors, artists and artisans to decorate them.

Even during this early period when violence was frequently the order of the day, Japan's delight in artistic expression was already conspicuous. Many Japanese who had little interest in Buddhist philosophy were enchanted by the artistic treasures and techniques that came along with the Buddhists, and wealthy families vied with one another in building and embellishing temples. As early as A.D. 640 there were several dozen Buddhist temples in Japan. Some of them are still preserved, notably the beautifully proportioned Golden Hall of the Horyuji monastery on the Yamato plain, which is probably the oldest wooden building in the world.

Along with Buddhism came a lesser infusion of Chinese Confucianism, which is a formalization of rules of ethics and behaviour said to have been handed down from remote antiquity. Among its central ideas is respect for superiors, especially parents. This is an outgrowth of the very ancient Chinese custom of ancestor-worship and stresses the reverence and devotion that children owe to their parents, for ancestors are the parents of parents. From earliest times the Japanese had also attached great significance to their ancestors, and even down to comparatively recent times the most important qualification for high public office was ancient and aristocratic lineage. The same family names remained prominent for centuries and when new families pressed to the forefront, they usually had, or claimed, descent from illustrious ancient names. Thus the Japanese welcomed the elegant treatment of the ancestor theme offered by Confucius and his followers.

Japan's own native religion, Shinto, was pushed into the background for a while. It went largely out of fashion at Court; even some emperors became pious Buddhists. But the lower classes, especially in the provinces, continued to worship their familiar nature-gods, and soon ingenious

theologians were reconciling Shinto and Buddhism. This was vital for Japan since the Imperial Family, the nation's symbol of unity, derived its sanctity from its descent from the Shinto sun-goddess. Little by little the two very different religions were intermingled. Ritual announcements by the emperor came to embody elements of both Shinto and Buddhism, as well as some features of Confucianism.

Japanese history has few examples of religious conflict, except when religious organizations become greedy for wealth or political power. Usually the various faiths managed to compose their differences without much trouble, and they sometimes did it in picturesque ways. One important step towards the reconciliation of Buddhism and Shinto was accomplished around A.D. 740 by the Buddhist monk Gyogi, an energetic and influential cleric who was as much interested in building irrigation works, bridges and public monuments as he was in deciding religious matters. To determine the propriety of the emperor's plan to erect a great statue of Buddha, he journeyed to Ise, the principal shrine of the sun-goddess, the supreme Shinto deity, and asked the goddess herself for her opinion. For seven days and seven nights he prayed at the door of the shrine. Finally the goddess answered in Chinese verse. The two religions, she

said in effect, were simply different forms of the same faith. So it was perfectly all right for her descendant, the emperor, to go ahead with his plan and to erect a statue of the Buddha.

Though the Japanese eagerly adopted and adapted Chinese religious, literary and artistic ideas, they did not accept so willingly the efforts of the imperial statesmen to impose on their loose and chaotic society the rigid Chinese system of central government. The initial move was made in A.D. 645 when the Emperor Kotoku, backed by the powerful Fujiwara clan, called the leading nobles together to hear an important announcement. It must have been a dramatic and touchy occasion that the noblemen had anticipated with mixed feelings. The proclamation was nothing less than a declaration of absolute monarchy by the emperor, and it was presently backed up by detailed decrees, called the Taika Reform, which copied almost exactly those theoretically in effect in T'ang China. All agricultural land, the basis of wealth in Japan, was declared the property of the throne, and it was to be allocated in small plots to the peasant households that cultivated it. The peasants in turn would pay part of their crop as taxes to the State and they would also be called upon for labour on public works. The system would be administered by officials appointed by the emperor and his ministers.

If this early version of State socialism inspired by China had been enforced suddenly and rigidly in Japan, it would probably have provoked a serious revolt by the powerful provincial barons, who held a tight grip on land and peasants. The fact that there was no revolt shows that the Taika Reform was not put into effect in one drastic step. Apparently, the new laws were enforced only when and where the Court and its allies were strong enough to enforce them. Some lands came under effective Court control while others, especially in regions distant from the seat of central authority, were left undisturbed. Few aristocratic landowners lost wealth or power because of the Taika Reform. Some of them gained a great deal, receiving rank and office in the new government commensurate with their former holdings; these noblemen naturally became enthusiastic supporters of the system.

Along with its provisions for land tenure, the reform created an elaborate hierarchy of Court ranks modelled on Chinese practice. Holders of rank were permitted to wear distinctive clothing at Court, and ranks above the fifth were allowed to enter the emperor's audience chamber. Such privileges came to be considered extremely important for their own sake, but there was also a solid economic side to the rank system. Members of the first five ranks got the income from specified amounts of the rice land owned by the State. In addition, they were allotted hundreds or even thousands of "sustenance households", which meant that they received the taxes which those peasant households would otherwise have had to pay to the government. When appointment as a government official was added to rank, the rank holder enjoyed an even greater income.

Rank-holding was almost always limited to the higher levels of the aristocracy, composed largely of junior branches of the Imperial Family, the heads of clans with ancient and illustrious lineage and certain aristocratic houses of Chinese or Korean origin. Some provincial magnates entered the lower ranks, but most of these were excluded from the charmed Court circle. The emperor's ministers, however, were careful to give provincial offices, with their emoluments, to clan chieftains who looked like potential trouble-makers, and these offices tended to become hereditary.

Besides its spotty enforcement, the system set up by the Taika Reform differed from its Chinese model in another important respect. In China, official appointments were commonly given to men who had passed rigorous written examinations. The subjects on which they were examined bore little relation to the duties to which they aspired, but the tests did help to select candidates who were intelligent and well-educated men. The Chinese bureaucracy manned by these scholar-officials, who might come from any class of the population, was remarkably forceful and efficient, and the opportunity that it offered to ambitious young men encouraged education and learning throughout China.

Scholarly Japanese who observed the Chinese bureaucratic organization were doubtless impressed by it, but if they tried to apply it in Japan, they did not succeed. Since custom dictated that long and prestigious ancestry was the prime requisite for high secular office, the Japanese appointment authorities who administered the Taika Reform proceeded in accordance with this tradition. Instead of testing aspirants for intellectual ability, they examined the candidates' genealogies to make sure that they were really descended from distinguished ancestors; the bureaucracy produced by this method was anything but efficient.

In spite of its many compromises, the Taika Re-

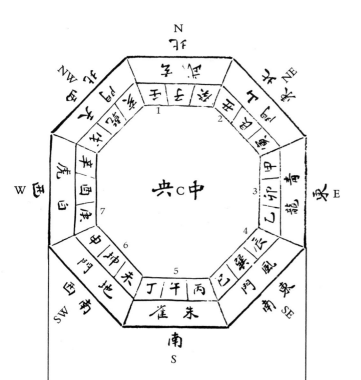

AN EVIL-PROOF PLAN

Geomancy, a pseudo-science of divination that originated in China, played on the superstitions of the early Japanese. In building a homestead, for example, the wise owner consulted a geomancer's "compass", like the one above, some of whose pronouncements are translated in the key below.

1. Good for building a store-house or a barn; receding ground at this point promises good luck. A lavatory does no harm.

2. Extension of the homestead here will bring destruction; a well promises ruin.

3. A store-house here is the agent of a second marriage and a gate of illness.

4. A gate here is a sign of comfort and cheer; a store-house, the source of prosperity.

5. Open space in this direction is the sign of peace; a well, that of eye diseases.

6. A pond here causes deaths from drowning or the intemperance of the master.

7. A stove facing east is apt to cause a fire; a Buddhist niche is the sign of good luck.

form did strengthen the central government and curbed the fractious independence of at least some of the provincial nobles. It greatly increased government revenue and led to improved communication with distant parts of the country. It created a valuable class of small landholders and stimulated the reclamation of many additional areas of rice land. Together with the influx of Chinese culture and technology it set Japan on the road to becoming an organized and reasonably unified nation.

Still lacking, however, was one essential for a country that was becoming increasingly stable—a fixed capital where government and imported arts, techniques and learning could flourish. When the eighth century began, Japan had no cities, only villages of thatched huts. The emperor's capital had been hardly more than a larger village, and it shifted its position whenever an emperor died, a step necessary to avoid the ritual uncleanness that, according to Shinto beliefs of the time, his death had caused. But the administrative machinery of the government had been growing, and the Taika Reform created a very large bureaucracy whose members, retainers and servants could not be moved easily. Furthermore, Chinese culture called for a fixed capital. The Chinese were not unconcerned with ritual uncleanness, but they had better ways of dealing with it than by moving away.

So in A.D. 710 a site for a permanent city was selected in the centre of the Yamato plain, which was then, as now, a green sea of rice fields. The choice was made in accordance with Chinese geomancy to determine whether the site would be lucky, and it may have been no accident that the chosen place was close to several powerful Buddhist monasteries.

The model for Japan's new capital and first real city, Nara, was the T'ang capital of Ch'ang-an.

Nara's builders copied its rectangular plan and laid out a grid of wide streets covering an area of 2½ miles by 3 miles, with the Imperial Palace north of its centre. Lining these avenues were the houses of noble families, and Buddhist temples and monasteries crowded thickly around the palace.

Nara became and long remained an impressive cultural centre, as well as headquarters for Japanese Buddhism. Much of Japan's national wealth, in the form of pious gifts from the Court and nobility, was poured into the city's Buddhist temples and monasteries. These ecclesiastical buildings, with their upward-curving, tiled roofs in the Chinese style, housed priceless treasures of paintings and sculpture. Their collections of books grew to respectable libraries that contained not only Chinese religious works but also many examples of Chinese secular literature and learning. Since Chinese culture was then the passionate concern of every Japanese with means and education, Nara quickly became the focus of fashion, attracting large numbers of pleasure-seekers as well as many more serious-minded people.

Though Nara gave Japan a brilliant capital, the government established there was not always effective. Its armies were so weak that they were often defeated by the Ainu in the north. Nearer home, the turbulent nobles and ambitious Buddhist clergy manœuvred ceaselessly to place their favourites in positions of great power. The climax of this power struggle came when the influence of Nara's numerous priests and monks had become so great that a member of the clergy even dared to aspire to the imperial throne. Following the abdication of the Empress Koken in favour of a young prince, a handsome and unscrupulous monk named Dokyo managed to get the ex-empress completely in his power, in much the same way as did the villainous Russian monk, Rasputin, who corrupted the Court of the last tsar. She sent the young emperor into exile; then she made herself empress again and named Dokyo as her chancellor-priest.

But Dokyo was not yet satisfied. He claimed that the great Shinto war-god Hachiman had declared that Japan would have peace for ever if he were made emperor. This was too much even for the empress. She sent a trusted emissary to Hachiman's shrine to ask the god if this were true. Hachiman's answer was that Dokyo, lacking imperial lineage, could not be emperor. The scheming monk soon fell from favour, and after the death of the empress in A.D. 770 he was banished from the Court.

This episode did not mark an end of Buddhist influence, however. Nara's temples and monasteries continued to grow, and their power made Nara an increasingly difficult place for the secular government. In A.D. 784 the Emperor Kammu decided that what was needed was a "priest-proof" city. Supported by the Fujiwara clan he gave the order to move the capital, first to near-by Nagaoka, which was soon abandoned as ill-omened, and later to the site of modern Kyoto. This was only about 25 miles from Nara, but the journey was difficult enough to reduce the influence of Nara's Buddhists.

The sun-goddess and other Shinto gods and spirits had been told of the move and they, if not the Buddhists, thought well of it. The new capital, laid out like Nara on a Chinese-style rectangular plan, was hopefully named Heian-kyo, meaning "the capital of peace and tranquillity".

Heian-kyo was not always peaceful and tranquil, but it was to be the centre for more than 300 years of a unique society that has fascinated everyone with even the most casual interest in Japan's past. It came to be called Kyoto ("the capital"), and under that name it remained the imperial capital of Japan for over a thousand years.

A VENERATED LAND

*Although the land of Japan has traditionally
been overpopulated, its natural beauty has
never been overrun. Rather, every available
plot of ground has been cherished. Forests
have been cultivated as carefully as rice fields
—each tree grows in its place because
someone intended it to be there.*

*Crowding has not cost Japan its beauty
because the people revere the land and
protect it. Some spots are famous for their
view of the moonrise, others for the
turbulence of surf churning around rocky
islets. Even Japan's violent aspects—its storm-
beaten coasts and fiery volcanoes—are goals
of pilgrimage. Honour for nature is so
ingrained in the Japanese that they, like the
monk above, would not fail to pause and
contemplate the colours of autumn leaves.*

PROTECTOR OR DESTROYER, A SEA
THAT HOLDS THE ISLANDS' FATE

*To the sea the Japanese owe their privacy.
A barrier against invasion, it has enabled
them to develop in relative isolation and to
produce a culture uniquely influenced by
the native environment. Ever present in these
surroundings is the sea itself, which breaks
the narrow land chain into almost 1,000*

islands, and provides such useful waterways as the Inland Sea (opposite page).

The waters that guard and serve Japan, however, sometimes batter it viciously with tidal waves. This capacity for good or evil is recognized in a unique ceremony that seeks omens for the future in the sea. Every 5th January, a large and a small rock in a bay near Ise are "wedded"—literally tied together by a straw rope (seen at the top of the picture above). At the end of a year's exposure to the ocean's violence, the rope is inspected: if broken, it signifies evil times; if unbroken, it foretells good days to come.

THE BEAUTY AND BOUNTY OF A
WELL-WATERED COUNTRYSIDE

*Japan's most abundant natural resource—and
the most vital one for its precious crops—is
fresh water. Its plentiful rainfall can take
the form of a typhoon's slashing sheets that
might leave up to 15 inches in a day, or the*

fine mists that settle gently over forests, such as those near Nikko (opposite). This heavy precipitation, lacing the countryside with rivers, streams and lakes, provides electric power and nourishes the world's most efficient farms. It also creates scenes of delicate, watery beauty, like the wooded waterfall at Kegon (above), that the Japanese portray in their painting, duplicate in their gardens and commemorate in their poems.

TEMPLES AND SHRINES THAT
REFLECT A UNIQUE REFERENCE
FOR NATURE

From the beginning, religion in Japan has
been inextricably bound to the land. The
first major faith, Shinto, was largely
predicated on nature, and trees, rocks and
streams were often worshipped as gods. Shinto
shrines, simple and·primitive, were placed
with an eye to scenic beauty in wooded

oves or on hill-tops. When Buddhism
ntered Japan in the sixth century, the
eling for nature permeated that religion
o. Buddhist pagodas, such as the one at
Nara shown opposite, were also built to
lend into secluded settings, and designed to
present aspects of nature. In the Nara

temple, the five swooping roofs symbolize
the five universal elements: earth, water, fire,
wind and sky. A Buddhist gravestone (above)
also reflects this intimacy with nature; set in
a quiet maple grove and flanked by stone
lanterns, it too is made up of sections
subtly echoing the sacred number five.

A SERENE VOLCANO: GRACEFUL
SYMBOL OF A NATION'S IDEAL

One natural feature has long stood as the
symbol of Japan: Mount Fuji, the tallest of
the country's 200 volcanoes. It combines
spectacular power (although it last erupted
some 300 years ago) with a gentle beauty

that conveys in its almost symmetrical cone the aesthetic purity prized by the Japanese.

In past centuries, the mountain was thought to be "the beginning of heaven and earth, pillar of the nation". Pilgrims scaled the heights chanting prayers, and miniature Fujis were worshipped in other parts of Japan. Today its religious role is much diminished, but a trip up Mount Fuji to watch the sunrise is still a cherished experience.

あきのよをへだてゝ

ふりにしひとも

あかぬこのよの

ちぎりかなひし

つかむゆめにみ

みえつる

おもひきやみねの

あらしのはげしさ

2

THE ELEGANT SOCIETY

THE BRILLIANCE OF CALLIGRAPHY *is shown in this decorative page from an early 12th-century anthology of poetry, in which the ornamental writing has been delicately brushed in ink on a flowered paper. In the Heian Age the art of calligraphy became a cult, and a person's character and breeding were usually assessed by the skill with which he handled his brush.*

When the Emperor Kammu established Japan's capital in the new city of Heian-kyo, he could not have foreseen the splendid success his action was to bring. Soon after the city was founded, in A.D. 794, it became a flourishing centre of culture, the home of a decorative society that for more than 300 years was like an endless pageant embellished with art, literature and music and spiced with titillating love affairs.

The site chosen for the capital was almost ideal for the nurturing of such a society. The gently sloping site was open to the south but enclosed on other sides by forested hills or mountains. The dangerous north-east direction, from which demons were most likely to swoop, was shielded by Mt. Hiei and its protective Buddhist monastery. Many fast-running streams brought clear mountain water, and a navigable river, the Yodo, provided convenient barge transportation to the sheltered Inland Sea that separated Honshu from the island of Shikoku.

Heian-kyo's plan, like that of the earlier capital, Nara, was copied from the great Chinese metropolis, Ch'ang-an, but with an important difference: by a royal edict, the areas in which Buddhist temples could be built were limited, and they were not permitted to cluster around the Imperial Palace, where their clergy might have too direct an influence on Court affairs. The Buddhist centre remained at Nara, a safe distance away, and during his lifetime the Emperor Kammu ruled his new capital himself, free of interference from either clerics or secular aristocrats. When he died in A.D. 806, however, the picture changed. Monks thronged to the capital, and temples sprang up throughout the city. More significantly, the later emperors fell increasingly under the political influence of that extraordinary family, the Fujiwara, who had begun their climb to power around the middle of the preceding century. Using the title of chancellor or regent, or sometimes no title at all, the Fujiwara soon became the real rulers of Japan.

The Fujiwara succeeded in fostering the growth of Heian-kyo and the development of its culture-orientated society, even though all around the city Japan struggled through dark and ignorant times. During the late eighth century and part of the ninth, when the city's characteristic culture was taking shape, most of Japan was still backward. The great bulk of its estimated five million people were simple peasants, and many provincial officials, priests and landowners were only slightly more cultivated. Conflict was frequent among them, and bloodshed was a common way of settling disputes. Moreover, for many years the warlike Ainu tribes on the northern frontiers were a serious cause of trouble.

Such a partly civilized country might be expected to have its central government safely situated in well-manned fortifications like the massive castles of medieval Europe, but this was not the case. The six-foot-high wall that girded Heiankyo was no more than a gesture, and it soon crumbled away. The Imperial Palace was a group of wooden buildings set in a spacious park and wholly unfortified. The only soldiers in the capital were the colourfully uniformed imperial guards, whose duties were ceremonial and whose military value was close to zero. Business-like weapons were seldom seen and hardly ever used. The most potent tools of competition were the fine-pointed brushes with which elegant courtiers vied with one another in writing subtle and intricate poems.

It is hard to explain how this island of calm and culture could flourish in a sea of ignorance and conflict. One influence may have been Buddhism; its doctrine of non-violence, though often ignored by the Buddhist priests themselves, governed many minds and must have had some gentling effect on politics. Possibly more effective was the political skill of the Fujiwara in substituting deft intrigue for simple sword-play.

From the ninth century to the 11th century the Fujiwara-dominated government was reasonably strong and effective, and Fujiwara ministers worked hard at politics and administration. Their family council settled conflicts within the clan and determined its policies towards the outside world. A large and efficient private bureaucracy managed the family's enormous wealth and also performed most of the practical functions of the central government. Agencies responsible to it collected taxes, appointed officials, regulated trade and controlled the Court.

To maintain their position, the Fujiwara had to support the emperor in full, impressive magnificence, while still keeping him strictly under their thumbs. This recurrent problem, which has baffled many a set of usurping politicians, they solved through marriage, in the manner pioneered by the Soga family centuries before. But the Fujiwara were more systematic and persistent. For generation after generation their leading branch produced an ample supply of beautiful, intelligent and prolific daughters. These charming instruments of statecraft were married to emperors or to emperors' sons. One of them normally became the empress, and her sons again were married to Fujiwara daughters. After a few generations of such inbreeding, which seems to have had no adverse genetic effects, the Imperial Family's ancestry was almost entirely Fujiwara.

But not entirely. The Imperial Family had, and the Fujiwara lacked, that long, thin genealogical thread leading back to the Shinto sun-goddess. Only a man who possessed this divine relationship could be emperor. The Fujiwara were careful to preserve the distinction, because the emperor's sanctity warded off attacks on the central government. Working through him and protected by his aura, they managed to govern Japan—firmly in the capital, much more loosely in the disorderly provinces—for more than three centuries.

Besides the political adroitness of the Fujiwara and the calming effect of Buddhism on Japanese politics, there is still another factor that helps to account for the long and peaceful existence of

A FIERCE PROTECTOR, *this wooden statuette about two feet tall, defends a Buddhist altar against demons. It was placed in a lavish mausoleum built in 1124 by Kiyohira, a Fujiwara general; the mausoleum houses the bodies of Kiyohira and his descendants.*

Heian-kyo: the enchantment of Japan's high aristocracy with its own version of Chinese culture.

Since the late sixth century, when Japan had begun to be deeply influenced by the cultural achievements of the great T'ang Dynasty in China, her aristocrats and scholars had admired everything Chinese. They wrote in Chinese, memorized Chinese poetry and avidly collected Chinese art. Large official embassies made the dangerous voyage to China and were joyously greeted when they returned laden with the treasures of a higher civilization. This intercourse ended soon after Heian-kyo was built, for the T'ang Dynasty, beset by revolts and invasions, was breaking up. After the Japanese completed a mission to China in A.D. 838, they did not plan on making another until A.D. 894, and it was abandoned when its leader decided that conditions on the mainland were too disorderly. Communication with China was broken off except for a trickle of scholars and traders.

The Japanese did not regret the loss. By this time they had absorbed a vast amount of Chinese culture and had created in their isolated capital a social life so delightful that most of the great noble families entitled by birth to participate in it had long since moved to Heian-kyo. There they stayed by passionate choice, abandoning the provincial strongholds that they might have used as power bases and using their wealth to patronize peaceful cultural pursuits. Their concentration in the capital, where any act of violence was considered bad form, gave Japan a kind of voluntary unity. Not until a whole new class of warlike aristocrats had arisen in the provinces in the 12th century did the wonderful Heian Age of peace come to a bloody end.

Few traces of Heian-kyo remain to recall this golden era. Even the city's name was changed. Modern Kyoto covers most of its site and preserves some of its chess-board street pattern, but except for a few tile-roofed temples, the wooden buildings of the original city have been swept away by repeated wars and fires during the rougher ages that followed. Although the city was physically destroyed and its enchanting life extinguished nearly 900 years ago, much of its rich and detailed literature has survived to tell of life in that ancient "Capital of Peace and Tranquillity". Because of its sensitive and delicate conventions, this literature has always had a strong appeal to the Japanese people.

The social life described so minutely in Heian writings involved perhaps no more than 3,000 of the city's 100,000 population. These select few, "dwellers among the clouds", were aristocrats closely associated with the Imperial Court. It was a closed group; for centuries it recruited almost no fresh blood. In its eyes the common people rated as semi-human and beneath notice except as curiosities. The lesser bureaucrats of the government were only a little better. Even provincial governors, who were often powerful and immensely rich, were despised as boors. But within the charmed circle of people of quality (literally "good people" in ancient Japanese) an enthralling game of manners and taste determined success at Court. Every move was made with utmost delicacy. A courtier's rise or fall might hinge on a single syllable of a poem. The exact shade of the paper on which a letter was written and the way the paper was folded carried a wealth of meaning. Perfume-blending was practised as a fine art, and socially prominent gentlemen were often recognized by a hint of their favourite scent drifting through a darkened room.

The sophisticated literature that illuminates the elegant society of the Heian Age was written almost wholly by women. The main reason for this was the enormous complexity of the Chinese system of writing that Japan's scholars had adapted to the Japanese language during the early years of Chinese influence and that was considered too difficult for women to learn. Chinese writing is made up of thousands of intricate characters that stand for words, not for sounds. This system worked well for Chinese because Chinese words are monosyllables that do not vary in form. But for Japanese, a language with a wholly different structure, it was agonizingly clumsy and had to be modified in ways that were also clumsy. The Chinese system of writing persisted, nevertheless, and for many centuries the mark of an educated Japanese man was his ability to write in Chinese characters.

The Japanese had handicapped themselves unnecessarily because even in ancient times their language was easy to write phonetically. It had only 47 syllables; if each were given a symbol to represent it, speech could be set down on paper with little difficulty. Two systems of syllabic writing, both called *kana*, were developed in the ninth century and came into wide use for informal purposes and popular literature. But writing in *kana* was beneath the dignity of high-ranking gentlemen and scholars who had been laboriously taught the complicated Chinese characters. When writing seriously they used them, and produced almost nothing of literary value.

The lively gentlewomen of Heian times suffered from no such limitation. They were not expected to learn the cumbersome Chinese, but they were highly literate in *kana*—which was sometimes called "women's writing". The brighter women—and some of them seem to have been almost too bright—wrote voluminously. Letters, diaries, novels and poems poured from their brushes. The best of this work is living literature today and makes the people and places it describes vividly alive too. Sprightly Heian authoresses tell of the routine of Court activity, describe its people and their manners, and recount tales of such diversions as poetry contests or even "cuckoo-viewing" expeditions, on which bevies of girls ventured into the countryside in ox-drawn carriages to listen to birdsongs, gather flowers and banter with whatever charming young men they chanced to encounter. Some of these writings have a serious side and rank among the finest works produced by any people in any age; they look beneath the gay exterior of Heian life and with startling insight lay bare the universal sorrows and anxieties that troubled even the seemingly carefree aristocrats who peopled the Imperial Court.

The hub of the colourful society shown in Heian literature was the emperor, who sometimes was no more than a child when he came to the throne. Genuinely revered as a religious and nationalistic symbol, but granted virtually no practical power, he spent his career performing the long, slow, sacred rituals considered necessary for the welfare of the country or acting as the central figure in the numerous Court festivities. Among the celebrations to which the emperor was expected to lend his presence was the annual Chrysanthemum Festival, when he and his nobles inspected the chrysanthemums in the gardens of the Imperial Palace. Following the rite of flower-viewing there was a banquet during which the emperor's guests composed poems and drank wine in which chrysanthemums had been steeped—a concoction believed to promote longevity.

Around the emperor a massive bureaucracy was mildly busy with functions of similar importance. Grave discussion and involved paper work concerned such details as the kind of carriage proper for a nobleman of a certain rank. The aristocratic officials in charge of this sort of activity were paid extremely well out of Court funds, but they spent little time at their work and often engaged substitutes to do it for them.

To modern eyes the perfumed "dwellers among clouds" who peopled the Court might not at first seem attractive. The men wore tiny patches of beard on the point of their chins. Both sexes covered their faces with white powder. The women shaved off their eyebrows and painted much heavier ones high on their foreheads. They also blackened their teeth; white teeth were considered glaring and hideous. They let their glossy black hair grow as long as possible: a girl was considered unusually lovely if her hair was abundant and longer than she was tall.

Clothing was incredibly elaborate, and nearly every detail was prescribed by Court regulations or etiquette. Men wore black laquered headgear that made them look like crested quail. Both men and women wore loose trousers, and on dress occasions a woman might wear over these as many as 12 silk robes of different colours, whose full sleeves were of varying lengths so that all would show a little at the wrists. When riding in carriages the girls hung their many-coloured sleeves over the sides for passers-by to admire. Each delicate shade of colouring had to be just right; if one was in slightly bad taste the whole Court heard about it.

From the diaries and novels of the women writers emerges a vivid picture of the city that formed the setting for this mannered way of life. Its avenues were broad and planted with trees, more like parks than thoroughfares. The principal avenue leading south from the enclosure of the Imperial Palace was nearly 300 feet wide, and the beauty of its willows was a favourite subject for poetry. Within the palace enclosure stood the city's most impressive building—the Great Hall of State, containing the dais on which rested the imperial throne. This hall, some 170 feet long, was a platform-like structure painted red and covered by a roof of dazzling blue tiles supported by 52 columns. Outside the palace area some religious structures had high roofs of green tile, but most of the buildings were one-storey with thatched or shingled roofs.

The homes of the nobility (others are seldom mentioned in literature) were built on main avenues in compounds covering several acres and were usually surrounded by low, white painted stone walls with carved and painted gates. A typical compound included a number of buildings. Besides the master's quarters there were separate structures housing his principal wife, his secondary wives and concubines, his children, relatives, retainers and servants. Like the temples and structures of State, these buildings were of wood. Rectangular and tastefully simple, they foreshadowed the austerity and understatement that would distinguish much of Japan's art and architecture through the ages. Each main building contained one large room that could be used as such for entertainments or divided into smaller rooms by movable screens and partitions. There were no windows. The outside walls consisted mostly of shutters that were taken down in warm weather and replaced by bamboo screens. The buildings within each compound were connected by long covered corridors, and a compound occupied by a growing household soon became a maze of passage-ways and courtyards.

Furnishings were few, as they are in Japanese homes today. In addition to the movable screens there was an occasional low table, braziers for heating and cushions for sitting on the floor. A platform called a *chodai*, about nine feet square and two feet high, stood in the centre of the large rooms. When furnished with mats and cushions and surrounded by curtains it served as a bed-chamber and provided a small amount of undependable privacy. Another common article of furniture was the *kicho*, a portable and attractively curtained frame, six feet high, with an unusual

function. It permitted a woman of quality to observe her surroundings and carry on a conversation while concealing herself from general view; those outside the curtains could see her only as a vague outline. The moment of commitment in a Heian love affair generally came when a lady permitted a gentleman to come behind her *kicho*.

Favourite locales for less-private social life were the gardens that adjoined the homes of the nobility. In these carefully landscaped grounds fast-running streams of clear mountain water fed artificial lakes, which sometimes contained small islands planted with pine trees. For major entertainments, elaborately carved and painted barges might be brought to navigate the little lakes. During "winding water banquets" ladies and gentlemen sat beside the circuitous streams, listening to music, fluttering their fans and flirting decorously. Now and again, a lacquered cup of wine floated by; guests in turn would pick it up, sip from it and recite an elegant poem before returning the cup to the flowing water.

One of the most revealing descriptions of Heian life is found in the *Pillow Book* written by Sei Shonagon, a light-hearted and highly observant young woman who was born about A.D. 966 and became a lady-in-waiting at the Court of the Empress Sadako. Sei Shonagon's *forte* was versification, and her book is full of poems packed with puns and literary allusions. The poems made a great impression and established Sei Shonagon as a leading wit at Court. They are so intricately constructed, however, that they defy translation; more interesting for modern readers are her impressions of very human Heian scenes. Writes Shonagon:

A girl is wearing an unlined robe of soft white stuff, full trousers, and a light purple mantle thrown across her shoulders with a

very gay effect. But she has some terrible malady of the chest. Her fellow ladies-in-waiting come in turns to sit with her, and outside the room there is a crowd of very young men inquiring about her with great anxiety: How terribly sad! Has she ever had such an attack before? and so on. With them no doubt is her lover, and he, poor man, is indeed beside himself with distress. But as likely as not it is a secret attachment, and fearful of giving himself away, he hangs on the outskirts of the group, trying to pick up news. His misery is a touching sight.

The lady binds back her beautiful, long hair and raises herself on her couch. Even now there is a grace in her movements that makes them pleasurable to watch. The empress hears of her condition and at once sends a famous reciter of the Scriptures, renowned for the beauty of his voice, to read at her bedside. The room is very small, and now to the throng of visitors is added a number of ladies who have simply come to hear the reading. At this exposed bevy of young women the priest constantly glances as he reads, for which he will certainly suffer in the life to come.

The high-born women described by Sei Shonagon, especially the young and pretty ones, were supposed to lead secluded lives, hiding themselves from prying eyes in their curtained *kichos* and showing their faces only to servants and close relatives. No doubt some of them lived up to this dull ideal, but to judge by contemporary literature, many were eager for any excuse to get outdoors to see and be seen. When a public ceremony or a lavish private entertainment was scheduled, the girls sallied forth in their carriages, surrounded by outriders and foot-retainers and often with gentlemen admirers riding alongside. Sometimes 500 carriages creaked along the capital's tree-lined avenues and tangled in sociable traffic jams while their passengers exchanged compliments, verses and song.

Days without entertainment dragged, but the nights were usually more interesting. "I like the feeling that one must always be on the alert", says Shonagon. "And if this is true during the day, how much more during the night, when one must be prepared for something to happen at any moment. All night long, one hears the noise of footsteps in the corridor outside. Every now and then the sound will cease in front of some particular door, and there will be a gentle tapping, just with one finger; but one knows that the lady inside will instantly have recognized the knock."

Shonagon must have heard many such tappings on her own door for she is expert in every detail of the clandestine but formalized Heian love affair. "It is important", explains Shonagon, "that a lover should know how to make his departure . . . One likes him to behave in such a way that one is sure that he is unhappy at going and would stay longer if he possibly could. He . . . should first of all come close to one's ear and in a whisper finish off whatever was left half-said in the course of the night. Then he should raise the shutters while he tells her how much he dreads the day that is before him and longs for the approach of night. Then, after he has slipped away, she can stand gazing after him, with charming recollections of those last moments. Indeed, the success of a lover depends greatly on his method of departure."

The preliminary move in such a Heian love affair would often have been made by letter. A young man, attracted by a beautiful girl, would compose a poem, weighing every syllable and trying to evoke an image that would make the lady eager to deepen the relationship. He carefully chose letter paper whose shade and texture lent themselves to the sentiments he wished to convey. Then he prepared his brush for the crucial step—the actual writing of the letter.

Mastery of calligraphy, the art of writing in flowing, cursive characters, was considered among the most important achievements of a Heian aristocrat; a person's handwriting revealed not only his education but also his social standing, character and mood. Sometimes a man would admire a lovely girl. write a poetic letter to her, entrust it to a messenger and wait with bated breath for her reply. If the girl's calligraphy lacked proper grace

and sensitivity, she sank below consideration, no matter how abundant her physical charms.

A more serious writer than Shonagon was Lady Murasaki Shikibu, whose romance, *The Tale of Genji*, is the great classic of Japanese literature. It is the first real novel in any language, as well as one of the longest. Written early in the 11th century, is has been the subject of praise, analysis and controversy, which started soon after the author's death and has continued ever since. Rarely, if ever, has a novel—or any work of literature except notable religious books—received such avid attention. In Japan alone it has been written about in more than 10,000 books. As early as the 13th century a 54-volume Japanese commentary appeared and in 1960 a Japanese publisher issued a *Tale of Genji Encyclopedia* that runs to some 1,200 large, closely printed pages.

The Tale of Genji well deserves this attention. Although it is written in 11th-century Japanese, as archaic as Anglo-Saxon (its European contemporary), Lady Murasaki's work has been skilfully translated into modern Japanese and also into English. Like few other books in world literature it acclimates the reader to an exotic way of life, remote in time and never duplicated, but intensely human nevertheless. Its characters and situations, spanning several generations, differ widely from chapter to chapter, and the scene shifts constantly —from the gay entertainments that enlivened the Heian Court to solemn ceremonies at mountain monasteries, to contests in painting, poetry and perfume-blending. One need not read the novel in its staggering entirety to enjoy it, however; the great book is full of short and wonderfully vivid episodes that can be read as self-contained entities.

The *Tale* includes many tales of love. Its hero, Prince Genji, the "Shining Prince", is the handsome son of an emperor who, says Lady Murasaki, lived "it matters not when", and the book is largely a psychological study of Genji's innumerable love affairs. Also recounted are the love affairs of some of his friends, relatives and descendants.

Prince Genji's first and principal wife was a woman with whom he had little to do, but since polygamy prevailed among the Heian aristocracy, he might properly engage himself in a great many amorous liaisons. His charm and position gave him a choice of any of the young ladies-in-waiting who attended his father's Court. But they did not interest him. He was always searching for distinctive qualities in women, and his quest led him to humble houses, neglected, weed-grown mansions or wherever a lovely girl of quality might be living in seclusion.

In one of the tenderest of the stories, Genji's search is rewarded during a trip to the sacred mountains where monks and hermits lived. While visiting a famous holy man he happens to find the daughter of a prince, a girl of ten, living with her grandmother who is a Buddhist nun. When the nun dies Genji takes the girl and raises her in his own house and eventually becomes her lover. This tale is told with such restraint that it throws no discredit on the Shining Prince. Indeed it has a happy ending: the girl becomes Prince Genji's favourite wife.

Not all is happiness in the world of Genji. To even the gayest inhabitants of the bright Heian society, illness and death bring frequent sorrow, and many of the love affairs in *The Tale of Genji* end tragically. One of Genji's charming young mistresses dies bewitched before his eyes. Frantically he tries to revive her, to drive away an evil spirit that he envisages as a tall, forbidding woman. But to no avail; the girl's small body grows cold. This horrifying scene haunts Genji, who falls sick himself and seems about to die. He recovers in time to order Buddhist rites to be held on the 49th day after the girl's death, when her soul is due to start its next lifetime, but even this gives him little solace. Writes Lady Murasaki:

> When he was secretly looking through his store for largess to give to the priests, he came upon a certain dress and as he folded it made the poem: "The girdle that today with tears I knot, shall we ever in some future life untie?" Till now her spirit had wandered in the void, but already she must be setting forth on her new lifepath, and in great solicitude he prayed continually for her safety.

Though advanced and highly refined in some ways, the Heian world reflected in *The Tale of Genji* was nevertheless full of gaps and contradictions. Education was largely a matter of learning to write in ponderous Chinese, memorizing innumerable poems and acquiring a brilliant polish in manners and etiquette. There was no science or other intellectual life and, after the breaking off of contact with China in the 800's, no interest in foreign countries. Even Japan's own past got negligible attention; the courtiers of Heian days lived in the present and used "old-fashioned" as a term of deep opprobrium. Costumes were elaborate, but food was simple and Heian literature hardly ever mentions it. Great effort was expended on gardens but little on houses, which could have been made much more comfortable.

In religious matters, the grossest superstitions marched side by side with lofty Buddhist philosophy. Divination, for example, was given serious attention, and the interpretation of omens as good or bad often played a decisive role in shaping government policies. Certain days were considered unlucky and on such days every effort was made to remain indoors and as inactive as possible. Even such a simple function as bathing or washing one's hair was put off until an auspicious date. Belief in demons, goblins and other noxious supernatural spirits was common, and there were

A LOFTY MONASTERY *below the peaks of Mt. Muro was initially built in the ninth century. Its monks lived close to the river and worshipped in temples that were situated on higher, more sacred land. In the Heian Age such monasteries acquired enormous tracts of tax-exempt land and thus placed a severe drain on the imperial economy.*

incantations, charms and spells in plenty to keep them at bay. In the Imperial Palace, for instance, the guards twanged their bow-strings at regular intervals to frighten away any evil spirits that might have invaded the royal precinct.

On the other hand, the writings of the Heian aristocrats sometimes made them seem sincerely pious; the Buddhist idea that the world is a place of universal suffering was deeply embedded in their minds. And yet the Heian nobility loved life too much to brood eternally on its evils. The women admired the attractions of men, and the men were always enchanted by the beauty of women. Hardly a page of *The Tale of Genji* lacks some delighted description of nature—of flowers or mist on still water or frost on pine needles. Though the Heian aristocrats seldom ventured far from their beloved capital, they watched every subtle change of the seasons, listened for the voices of birds and insects, took fearful pleasure in thunder and typhoons. But while much of their literature portrays them as smiling often, a sense of gloom and melancholy underlies their more serious writings, for they recognized that evils existed and portended coming difficulties.

The charmed world of the Heian aristocracy had begun to wane by the start of the 11th century. Buddhist sages had long been warning that "the latter days of the law", when the Buddha's teachings would lose their benefit, were close at hand. Many Heian courtiers of the day looked towards the future with ever increasing apprehension. Troubles were certainly multiplying. They did not come from any mystical source, however, but from the slow deterioration of the political and economic base that supported the capital city.

The roots of this difficulty led back to the seventh century, when the Taika Reform of Emperor Kotoku tried to set up the Chinese system of land ownership by the State. This system, which required peasant cultivators of the land to pay taxes directly to the emperor's government, never went into full operation in Japan, chiefly because the central government was never strong enough to establish it firmly. Many provincial magnates continued to control productive land and refused for various reasons to pay taxes. As time passed, these provincial estates, which might be made up of many scattered parcels of land, gained formal exemption from taxes and services, and so did land that emperors granted to favourite courtiers and religious foundations. Each loss of taxable farmland reduced the income and influence of the imperial Court.

Even more damaging to the Court was the custom of "commending" taxable land to tax-free overlords. This practice grew out of the plight of peasants who held their land directly from the State and not from the powerful estate-owners. For these poor farmers, no local aristocrats or stewards stood ready to intercede against imperial tax-collectors, who were often corrupt and oppressive, or against imperial agents who conscripted men for labour and military service. The draft for troops was especially dreaded. A young conscript had to supply his own food, clothing and weapons, and the burden of having a son in the army was often enough to ruin a peasant family.

There was a simple way out of this precarious position. The peasant could entrust his land to a tax-exempt nobleman or temple; he then received the right to continue to cultivate it in return for payments that were less than the taxes and services that he had been paying to the State. If the new patron was strong enough, he protected the peasant from grasping officials and kept his sons out of the army. There were many variations of this transaction, some of them very complicated, but they all took land from the tax rolls of the central government.

While taxable lands shrank, private manors increased in size, number and wealth. Some of them belonged to rich Court nobles, especially the Fujiwara, who were the richest of all; others were the personal estates of the many branches of the Imperial Family. Part of this growth came from adventurous pioneering outside Court control. Many a youth of good family, who saw no prospect of keeping up with the fashionable society of the Court, went into the provinces to increase an insufficient inheritance and never came back. Young men of peasant origin did the same, leaving their homes in settled districts for the wild frontiers where they saw hope of a better life. Neither nobles nor peasants on the frontier paid much attention to orders from the capital.

Japan was expanding. Every year more rice lands were brought under cultivation, especially in northern areas of the main island of Honshu. New land was theoretically the property of the State, but much of it fell into the hands of provincial barons, who were not at all like the perfumed and culture-obsessed aristocrats of the imperial capital. They were exceedingly tough, schooled in traditions of warfare against unsubdued Ainu and against an unruly frontier population made up of Japanese settlers, outlaws, aborigines and the offspring of all these elements. A similar situation existed in southern Kyushu, where barbarians called Kumaso had held out for centuries against Japanese conquest. Even in long-settled districts local magnates organized private armies to protect themselves or to take land from their neighbours. Buddhist temples and monasteries followed suit; they armed their monks or engaged mercenaries to seize new land or revenues.

The central government, which meant in effect the Fujiwara family, fought a long rearguard action against the loss of taxable State land and the increase of provincial independence. As its income and influence diminished it came to depend on alliances with warlike provincial families, especially on one called the Minamoto, which headed a powerful league of warriors and was known as "the teeth and claws of the Fujiwara". Another family, the Taira, helped the Fujiwara to suppress for a time the pirates that had long infested the Inland Sea. Gradually, the fighting men of the provinces gathered around the banners of either the Minamoto or the Taira, thus dividing most of the nation into two warlike leagues.

Early in the 11th century the provinces were in turmoil, with private armies battling each other and defying the forces of the central government. The highways were plagued by bandits; the seas swarmed with pirates. Often disorder penetrated into the Capital of Peace and Tranquillity itself. Robbers broke into noblemen's homes or set the wooden buildings on fire. Armed monks from the mountain monasteries swept through the city's stately avenues and from the gates of the Imperial Palace threatened the Fujiwara-controlled government. Major revolts, however, were harshly suppressed by armies organized and led by the Minamoto. Since they had little piety, they were especially good at chasing clerical hoodlums back to their monasteries. But disorder increased; much of the city was burned to the ground and never rebuilt. Large sections lapsed into wilderness infested with outlaws and robbers.

Worst of all, the Fujiwara seemed to have lost their political magic. Branches of the family, which had grown enormously, began to plot against one another, and at a critical time the leading branch failed to produce enough daughters to keep all the scions of the Imperial Family safely supplied

with Fujiwara wives. In 1068 the Emperor Go Sanjo (Sanjo II) came to the throne. His mother was not a Fujiwara, and so he had no filial obligations to the long-dominant family. Furthermore, he was no helpless youth. He was 35 years old, a vigorous, intelligent man, and determined to rule without Fujiwara control.

This he succeeded in doing during a reign of four years, though disorder in the provinces continued and increased. Then he abdicated, leaving the throne to his son Shirakawa. This action freed him from the burden of ceremony that consumed nearly all the titular emperor's time and energy and allowed him to govern fairly effectively in his son's name. Go Sanjo died a year after his retirement. His son continued to rule for a while as emperor, then abdicated in turn and became a monk.

This curious institution of government by an officially retired ruler characterized the closing century of the Heian Age. The titular emperor and his Court busied themselves with elaborate religious rituals while the Retired Emperor ruled from offices set up in his private residence. Meanwhile confusion and disorder continued to grow. Sometimes there was more than one Retired Emperor contending for power, and as central authority became more chaotic the Minamoto, the Taira and other warrior clans fought one another with increasing ferocity in their struggle for power, wealth and prestige.

With turmoil and defiance mounting throughout Japan and more and more land being seized by provincial barons, the income that had supported the Court and its "dwellers among the clouds" in elegance for over three centuries was drastically reduced. By the middle of the 12th century the brilliant social life of the capital had lost its lustre, and the Heian golden age gave way to a dark era filled with the clash of arms.

PRINCE GENJI, *shielded by an umbrella and preceded by an attendant, sets out to visit a lady frien*

TALES OF COURTLY LOVE

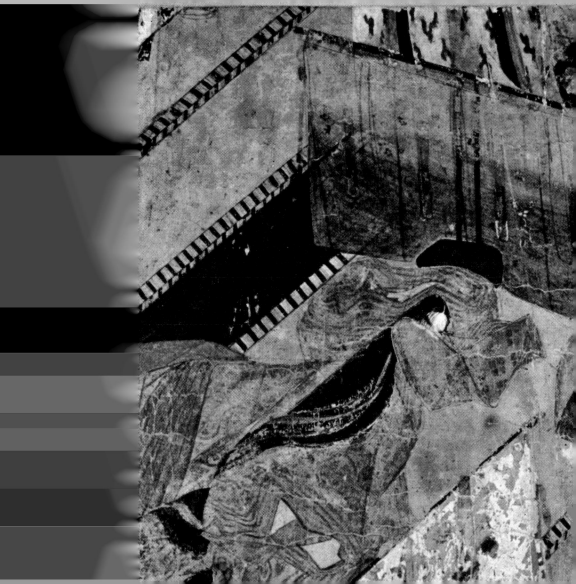

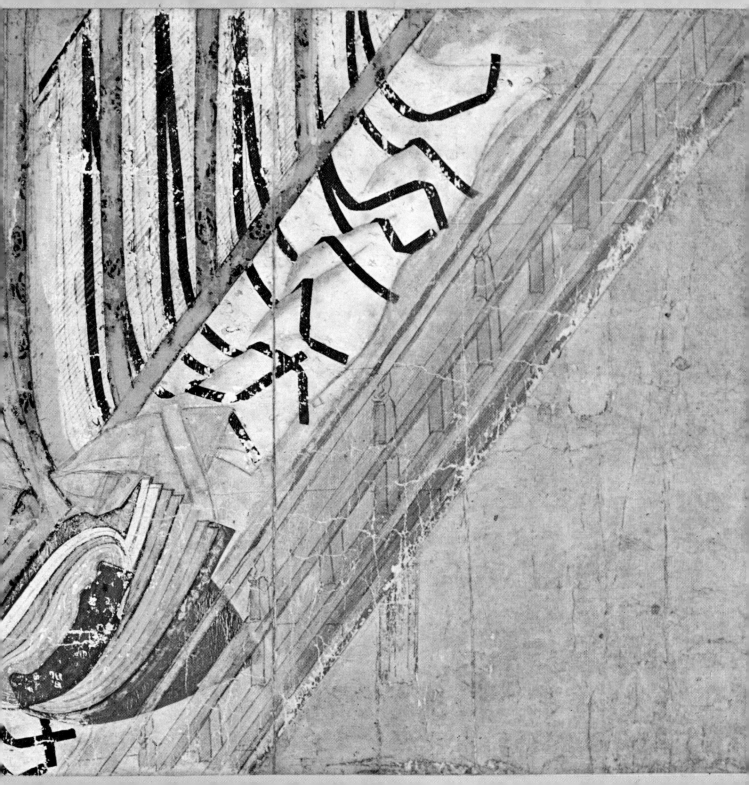

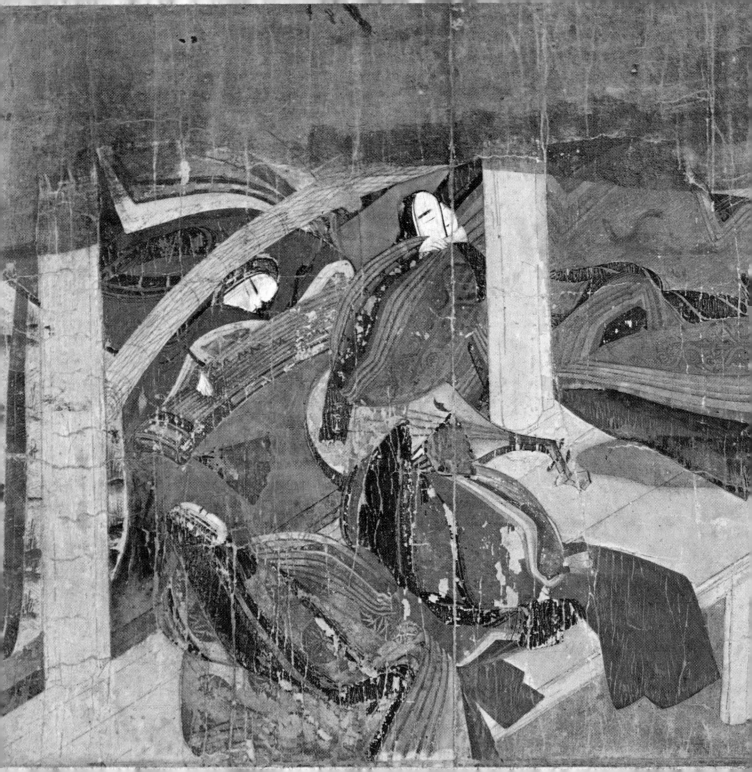

A DIPLOMATIC GAME OF "GO" TO WIN A PRINCESS'S HAND

For a long time Kaoru was disconsolate over Oigimi's death. But, while love was a matter of the heart in Heian Japan, matrimony was usually political. So, when the emperor proposed a marriage with his daughter, Kaoru swallowed his unhappiness and accepted.

The emperor's offer was made with characteristic Heian delicacy. His Majesty challenged Kaoru to a round of "go", a traditional Japanese board game, hinting vaguely to Kaoru that "you shall have a present if you win, and a handsome one too"—a veiled reference to his daughter. In this scene the emperor, seated opposite Kaoru (who sits at the bottom right), places one of his men on the "go" board. The emperor conveniently lost the game; Kaoru, diplomatically acknowledging his unworthiness to become the emperor's son-in-law, plucked a chrysanthemum from the imperial garden and handed it to the emperor while he recited an

3

RISE OF THE SAMURAI

Like a dark cloud blotting out the sun, a turbulent era of bloodshed and almost incessant warfare followed the golden Heian Age. Within the Imperial Court gentle artistry and refinement were a continuing ideal, but all around brutal violence flourished and at times shattered the serenity of the Court itself. Now feats of arms took precedence over poetry contests and "cuckoo-viewing" excursions into the countryside, and a new kind of man—the mounted knight in armour—clattered on to the scene to win dominance over the elegant courtier of an earlier age.

The rise of the fighting man had begun in the 11th century, as the power of Japan's central government gradually eroded. Its Fujiwara ministers had attempted to maintain their influence by making alliances with the powerful military factions, especially those of the Minamoto and Taira clans. But by the middle of the next century conflict among these ambitious leagues intensified, and the warrior became supreme; before the 12th century was over he had firmly imposed on Japan a system of military rule that was to persist, with various modifications, for some 700 years.

A reasonable date for the dawn of Japan's militaristic feudal age is 1156. In that year war between the Minamoto and Taira leagues swept for the first time over the unfortified, ungarrisoned capital that came to be called Kyoto. But the forces that led to the war and were instrumental in shaping feudalism had long been gathering. As early as A.D. 946, in the heyday of Fujiwara rule, an official had reported: "Many make lawless use of power and authority; form confederacies; engage daily in military exercises; collect and maintain men and horses under pretext of hunting game; menace district governors; plunder the common people; violate their wives and daughters; and steal their beasts of burden and employ them for their own purposes, thus interrupting agricultural operations". He recommended that "persons who enter a province at the head of parties carrying bows and arrows shall be recognized as common bandits and thrown into prison".

If any such order were issued, it was never enforced, and as the effectiveness of centralized authority gradually diminished, disorder increased

A MOUNTED SAMURAI, *arrayed in armour and carrying a sword, a bow and a quiver of arrows, plunges into the sea in this detail from a painting of a 12th-century battle between the rival Taira and Minamoto clans.*

A FEUDAL ESTATE, *owned by two samurai brothers, straddles a river in this 13th-century map. The brothers lived on opposite banks in manor houses with high peaked roofs (centre, top and bottom), and their holdings included cottages and markets.*

in the provinces. When landholders found they could no longer depend on royal officials for protection against outlaws or predatory neighbours, they armed their sons and retainers and put themselves under the leadership of chiefs renowned for fighting ability.

At the start of the 12th century these armed groups were numerous but remained small and local because the power and intrigues of the Fujiwara family, reaching out from the capital, kept them from growing big enough to threaten the central government. But the violent trend of the times was against small groups; those that did not make powerful alliances were almost sure to be subjugated and despoiled. To gain additional strength for defence or offence, the warrior-chiefs of each small region banded together and offered their combined services to more important lords. In return for this support the lords agreed to pro-

tect the minor chiefs and their followers and to share with them any booty that they might win. The lords in turn pledged allegiance to still loftier noblemen who were members of some ancient and mighty family, or at least claimed to be. These step-by-step bonds of allegiance were strikingly similar to the feudal alliances that developed in Europe during the centuries of political chaos after the fall of Rome. And in Japan, as in medieval Europe, these alliances supplied the basis for a crude but effective scheme for enforcing some kind of order in a turbulent time. They are a natural response to the failure of authorized government to provide protection.

As the Heian Age drew to a close, most warrior-landholders had become associated, frequently through several stages of allegiance, with the two great military families, the Minamoto and the Taira. These families ranked lower than the Court nobles, though each claimed descent from early emperors. Both had numerous branches, some of which were bitter rivals for land and power and only too apt to desert to the other side. Both had well-established representatives in all long-settled parts of Japan, and branches of both families had followed the frontier as it advanced into eastern and northern Honshu. In many places Minamoto and Taira estates lay side by side, mingled with those of lesser provincial families that gave allegiance to one or the other.

With the growth of a feudal system based on personal and family loyalty came the appearance of that most famous of Japanese types, the samurai, or gentleman warrior. "Samurai" means "one who serves", and the samurai were soldiers who served personal chiefs. Some were wealthier than others, but no matter what their economic circumstances, all were theoretically bound by a code that demanded absolute loyalty to their immediate superiors in the feudal chain of command. Nothing was supposed to interfere with this devotion, neither love of wife and children nor duty to one's parents. Least of all should the fear of death affect a man's fidelity to his feudal leader. In a Japanese tale dating from the 12th century, one noble warrior puts into vivid words the samurai's utter contempt for death: "...I spurred my horse on frowning precipices, careless of death in the face of the foe. I braved the dangers of wind and wave, not reckoning that my body might sink to the bottom of the sea, and be devoured by monsters of the deep. My pillow was my harness, arms my trade...".

The wealthier samurai fought on horseback, clad in helmet and flexible armour made of narrow steel strips held together by cords or thongs. These fierce, grim, aristocratic horsemen resembled outwardly the knights of medieval Europe, but, except for their devotion to their overlords, the

inward principles that motivated them were quite different. The ideal of chivalry and the glorification of womanhood that underlay European knighthood had no counterpart among the samurai. Nor were the samurai inspired by religious fervour. As a samurai warrior plunged into battle he was no crusader invoking heavenly aid in his war cries. Instead, he sought to strike terror in his enemies by shouting his own prowess and the names and exploits of his illustrious ancestors.

Eventually, the warrior caste acquired characteristics that set it widely apart from the rest of the population, and no one below samurai rank was permitted, at least in theory, to carry the supreme weapons of Japanese warfare, the long, two-handed swords that were revered almost like sacred objects. But the full mystique of the samurai had not taken shape by the middle of the 12th century when the power struggle between the Minamoto and Taira factions was approaching a climax. The tradition of personal loyalty, however, was already strong, creating a chain of power that reached up from individual warriors through subordinate chiefs and great lords to the Minamoto and Taira. The private councils of these two families became the strongest law-making and law-enforcing bodies in the land.

An agreement between the Taira and Minamoto, perhaps sealed by a series of marriages, might have brought peace to the entire country, but such a *détente* hardly suited the belligerent spirit of the times, which favoured fighting to every bitter end. No feeling of patriotism urged the factions to make peace for the nation's sake. Except for the vague, semi-religious attachment that all Japanese felt towards the Imperial Family, there existed as yet no concept of Japan as a nation.

The Minamoto were the first of the two great warrior leagues to win strong influence at Court; after the decline of Fujiwara control the family moved into Kyoto and secured many high offices. This rise to power was resented by the Taira, and in a series of intrigues and battles they sought to dislodge the Minamoto from the capital. In 1156 full-scale war between the rival families erupted in Kyoto itself, and the city that for more than 300 years had been a sanctuary of culture and elegance became the scene of great cruelty and destruction. Samurai warriors and common soldiers of both sides burned palaces and slaughtered the inhabitants. Most of the prisoners were executed, often beheaded, though capital punishment had long been abolished at Court because of Buddhism's stress on non-violence. Early in the struggle the captured chief of the Minamoto family was condemned to death by the Taira, and his own son was ordered to kill him. The son refused, but a Minamoto officer did the deed rather than have it done by a hated Taira. Then he killed himself.

Grisly descriptions of warfare between the two factions abound in the literature of the time. One tale describes a Minamoto raid on the palace of a retired emperor who was in league with the Taira: "Wild flames filled the heavens, and a tempestuous wind swept up clouds of smoke. The nobles, courtiers and even the ladies-in-waiting of the women's quarters were shot down or slashed to death. . . . When they rushed out, so as not to be burned by the fire, they met with arrows. When they turned back, so that they would not be struck with arrows, they were consumed by the flames. Those who were afraid of the arrows and terrified by the flames even jumped into wells in large numbers, and of these, too, the bottom ones in a short time had drowned, those in the middle were crushed to death by their fellows, and those on top had been burned up by the flames".

From such orgies of blood and arson the Taira

JAPAN'S FIRST SHOGUN, *Minamoto Yoritomo became militar dictator in 1185, when he vanquished the leaders of th rival Taira clan. From his capital at Kamakura, he set i a system of military government that lasted almost seve centuries. He is shown in full Court dress, holding a scep tre in his right hand, in this 13th-century wood sculptur*

emerged the victors. In 1160 Kiyomori, the Taira leader, seized control of the Imperial Family and the central government. Minamoto survivors retreated beyond his reach, mostly to the eastern provinces in the region around modern Tokyo, a frontier area where the authority of the Kyoto government had never been strong. There they waited for the next round of war.

Kiyomori was a clever politician who understood better than most warriors how to manipulate the intricate mechanism of the ancient Court government. He took part in the capital's social life, which remained nearly as frivolous as it had been during the Heian Age, and made friends with frosty Fujiwara nobles, who still held numerous posts at Court. He even married a daughter into the Imperial Family; the Emperor Antoku, who came to the throne in 1180 at the age of two, was his grandson. Apparently Kiyomori's objective was to make the Imperial Family a Taira appendage so that the Taira could govern indefinitely in the imperial name, as the Fujiwara had done.

This policy failed because it copied the dead past and did not recognize the capital's impotence in this new age of the fighting man's supremacy. By the second half of the 12th century the emperor's Court had become little more than a symbol. The only reality was armed force, and it was controlled by fierce warrior families scattered over Japan. When Kiyomori and other Taira leaders made the mistake of settling down in Kyoto, they gave themselves over to the pleasures of the Court and tended to lose touch with the provincial barons. The Taira and their followers were never able to rally forces sufficient to subdue the eastern provinces—despite many gallant attempts—and Minamoto survivors gathered there like a thundercloud for a bloody come-back.

The Minamoto struck in 1180 under the leadership of Yoritomo, who ultimately proved to be one of Japan's greatest statesmen. The struggle see-sawed to and fro across the country in an orgy of slaughter and devastation. Even after the Taiara leader, Kiyomori, died in 1181, the war raged on.

By 1183 two Minamoto armies threatened the Taira in Kyoto itself. Late in the summer of that year the demoralized Taira abandoned the capital and retreated westwards with the child-emperor Antoku. But they were not able to take with them the support of the ex-emperor Go Shirakawa who, although officially retired, had continued to rule in Antoku's name. He defected to the Minamoto and encouraged their generals to pursue and punish the Taira as rebels. This imperial blessing, coming from a descendant of the sun-goddess, produced important results; although Go Shirakawa had no real power, many wavering warrior-chieftains joined the Minamoto faction because the Retired Emperor's support made that cause seem the legitimate one.

The Taira were finally crushed in a great naval battle fought on the Inland Sea in 1185. The Emperor Antoku, then seven or eight years old, was drowned along with most of his entourage. The destructive five-year war was over, and out of it was to grow the strongest government the country had yet known.

Yoritomo, the Minamoto leader, saw in the samurai's feudal code of loyalty and service to his lord a basis for governing the whole country through a military dictatorship. Before he could put his plan into effect he had to suppress many rivals in his own faction, including his brother, who was one of his best generals. As one ambitious rival after another was disposed of, the country gradually quietened down, and Yoritomo began to build the structure for his rule. From the Retired Emperor Go Shirakawa (now acting in the name of the child who was Antoku's successor) he extracted the authority to appoint constables and stewards in the provinces. This grant of power, given very reluctantly, was the keystone of the new scheme of government. Constables were local military chiefs, and when Yoritomo appointed his loyal henchmen to these offices, he went far towards securing military control of the provinces. Stewards were managers of estates who in the course of time often became their effective proprietors. By the judicious appointment of stewards, Yoritomo and his loyal vassals gradually won possession of a large proportion of Japan's most productive land.

With the fall of the Taira before him as an example to be avoided, Yoritomo did not make the mistake of moving to Kyoto, where he and his tough soldiers would be exposed to the blandishments of the Imperial Court. Instead he established his headquarters in the small town of Kamakura near the mouth of Tokyo Bay, where the Minamoto maintained a shrine of the war-god Hachiman. There experts from Kyoto helped him to build up what amounted to a private government with a small but efficient bureaucracy. He headed it himself as *Seii-taishogun* (barbarian-suppressing commander-in-chief), a title conferred by the emperor. Directly below him were an administrative council, a system of Courts and an all-important office called the *samurai-dokoro*. The name had originally meant "service room", a place where a nobleman's servants waited, then it came to designate a guardroom for armed retainers. Under Yoritomo it became an office to deal with all the affairs of military men, allocating duties and privileges, recommending promotions and rewards, determining punishments and even regulating a soldier's family and personal behaviour. Since the feudal warriors of Japan had become the only class that really mattered, keeping them strong, orderly, contented

and firmly attached to the régime was the most important task of statecraft. The *samurai-dokoro* was thus more than an army central office; it was a source of power.

The shogun and his new administration, although now the strongest authority in Japan, were not the country's formal government. Theoretically the Imperial Court at Kyoto and its officials still had this function, and Yoritomo was careful to preserve the illusion. But everyone with government business quickly learned that nearly all real power resided in the shogun's headquarters at Kamakura, the *Bakufu*. Its judges decided lawsuits and did so much more fairly and honestly than the emperor's Courts had ever done. The *Bakufu* executives appointed provincial officials and managed public works such as harbours, land reclamation and irrigation improvements. When disputes arose among the feudal lords or their samurai, the *samurai-dokoro* usually settled them with a minimum of bloodshed.

Yoritomo's reign as shogun was not always peaceful; his generals fought many campaigns against recalcitrant barons, mostly in remote parts of the country. The generals always won, and Yoritomo divided the estates of the vanquished among his loyal vassals. He died in 1199, and since the two sons who succeeded him in turn were less able than their father had been, his government would probably have fallen apart except for his strong-minded widow, Masa-ko. This extraordinary woman had shown her mettle as a young girl when she eloped with Yoritomo on the very day that she was scheduled to marry another man. After her husband's death she intrigued so skilfully that members of her father's family, the Hojo, eventually emerged as regents in complete control of the office of shogun.

For well over a century the Hojo family controlled Japan, and the shogun was reduced to a figure-head. During this period the country's government was an extraordinarily complicated maze. Its titular chief was the emperor at Kyoto, but his powers—such as they were—were actually administered by a Retired Emperor, usually his father. The Retired Emperor in turn delegated imperial power to govern to the military shogun at Kamakura, and the shogun himself was dominated by a Hojo regent.

This long chain of delegated powers held together remarkably well. From time to time, to be sure, an emperor would conspire with ambitious noblemen to recover real power, but all such conspiracies were crushed by the Hojo regents without difficulty. In a way the Hojo even found the uprisings helpful; by giving the confiscated estates of the conspiring nobles to devoted vassals, they strengthened the feudal loyalties that supported their power.

For much of the 13th century Japan was relatively prosperous and tranquil under the strong rule of the Hojo regents, which was remarkably beneficent for its day. Population increased; towns began to grow into cities; trade with China increased, bringing wealth and new ideas to Japan. Also, by mid-century the samurai code of honour had begun to develop from a simple set of feudal loyalties into a powerful ethical code that is still influential in Japan, and most of the trappings of war that would identify a samurai for centuries to come had taken shape.

Although military rule had brought order inside Japan, trouble was building up overseas, and ultimately it would put the samurai caste to its severest test. In the early 1200's fierce and aggressive Mongols burst out of Central Asia on a campaign of conquest that terrorized most Asiatic lands and eventually a good part of Eastern Europe as well. With growing apprehension the Japanese watched Mongol armies overrun China under the leadership of Genghis Khan and his descendants. When they saw Korea also fall to the conquerors, they realized that an attack on Japan might not be far away.

In 1268 the Great Khan of the Mongols, Genghis Khan's grandson Khubilai, sent an ambassador to the "King of Japan", whom he addressed as "the ruler of a small country". He suggested that friendly intercourse with China was desirable and pointed out diplomatically that lack of such relations might lead to war. The Hojo government at Kamakura realized that this was a veiled threat, but it was in no mood to yield. It sent the Mongol ambassador back to China without an answer and treated later ambassadors in the same silently defiant way. Such defiance could not go unchallenged, and the Hojo regent perceived that the first attack would probably strike at the island of Kyushu, a convenient base for an assault on the main island of Honshu. He ordered coastal defences to be strengthened and warned the warriors of Kyushu to stay on the alert. Meanwhile his spies kept close watch on Korea, from which an invading force would most likely sail.

The Mongols, being Central Asian horsemen, knew nothing about seafaring, but they forced the Koreans to build and man a great fleet of some 450 ships. In November 1274, the armada, carrying 15,000 Mongol troops, sailed out into the stormy Korea straits and took the small islands of Tsushima and Iki, whose Japanese garrisons died to the last man. Then the fleet continued to Kyushu and landed at Hakozaki Bay on the north coast.

Hurrying into battle came the local samurai. They knew that great armies dispatched by the *Bakufu* were moving to support them, but not waiting for help they threw themselves recklessly on the dreaded Mongols, shown by contemporary Japanese artists as hairy subhumans. The samurai enjoyed the benefit of fighting on their home grounds, but in every other respect were at a considerable disadvantage. They had never faced a foreign enemy, and in their civil warfare they used hardly any military formations. The high-ranking warriors generally fought opponents of equal ranks in formalized single combat. The Mongols, on the other hand, were accomplished tacticians, manœuvring skilfully in tight formations. Their powerful cross-bows shot bolts that outranged Japanese arrows, and they brought artillery of a sort: catapults that hurled flaming projectiles and explosive missiles. Against this formidable military machine the Japanese could muster only their valour and their deadly, cherished swords.

The battle was inconclusive. At dusk the Japanese withdrew behind earthworks, and the Korean seamen, not liking the look of the weather, persuaded the Mongols to board the ships. That night a storm broke, sank many of the ships and blew the remnants of the fleet back towards Korea.

Soon after this abortive invasion, Khubilai Khan sent another embassy, this time ordering the "King of Japan" to come to the Mongol capital of Peking and do homage. It was an ultimatum. The Imperial Court at Kyoto was terrified, but Kamakura's resolute *Bakufu* rejected all thought of yielding and underlined its decision in the strongest way it could think of: by lopping off the heads of the Mongol ambassadors. This was the ultimate insult, and it was thrown in the face of an enemy people whose conquests now reached from the China Sea all the way across the continent of Asia to Arabia, and whose horsemen had ravaged as far west as Hungary.

The Japanese knew only too well that another and stronger Mongol attack would come, and they began to prepare for it with a unity that the country had never shown before. To hinder the charges of the Mongol landing parties, land-owners on Kyushu were ordered to build a wall around Hakozaki Bay, on whose sheltered shores the enemy was again expected to land. Small, manœuvrable warships were built to attack the clumsy Mongol transports, and crews were trained to handle them. A census was taken of all men on Kyushu able to bear arms so that they could be called up immediately to repel invaders, and warlike barons all over Japan were told to keep their troops ready for battle at a moment's notice. Weapons were stockpiled; the Court at Kyoto gave up luxuries to save resources for defence. Even the pirates who terrorized the Inland Sea—some of whom were samurai whose lands touched its shores—joined enthusiastically with government forces in naval manœuvres.

The respite lasted for five years while the Mongol conquerors were busy mopping up remnants of resistance in southern China. Then Japanese spies brought word that large-scale preparations were under way. Again the Koreans had been ordered to build ships, a thousand of them this time, and a Mongol army of 50,000 was marching towards the shore of the Korea straits. Simultaneously an even bigger fleet was reported gathering in the south of China to embark an army of 100,000 men. Although the spies may have inflated the numbers, there seems little doubt that this was the largest sea-borne invasion force in history until modern times.

Early in the summer of 1281 the Mongol fleet sailed from Korea and made for Kyushu, as before. The first troops landed on the 23rd June at many places on the north coast, including the walled shores of Hakozaki Bay. The fleet from China reached Kyushu soon after and landed most of its soldiers farther west. With a characteristic contempt for death, the Japanese attacked at once; their small boats did great damage, armed crews boarding the enemy transports or setting them on

THE IMPERIAL RESIDENCE *moved four times in Japan's history. The first capital, Nara, was abandoned in A.D. 784. The emperor moved briefly to Nagaoka and then to Heian-kyo (Kyoto). By 1192 a shogun had taken over Japan's administration and ruled from Kamakura and later Edo. Since 1869 Edo, renamed Tokyo, has been both the imperial and the administrative capital.*

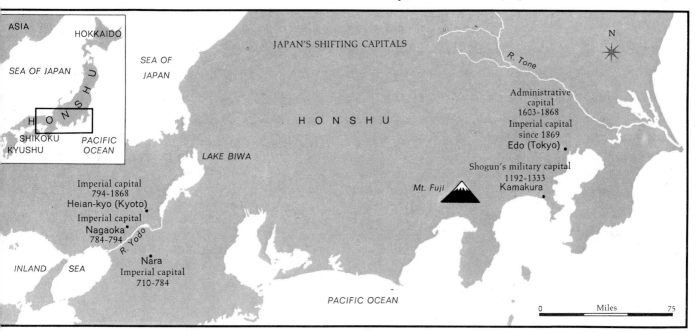

fire. The most potent weapon of the Mongols, the paralysing terror that they had inspired across much of the 13th-century world, had no effect at all on the Japanese.

Great armies were streaming towards the battlefield, the samurai leaders racing each other to get there first. Priests and monks in monasteries throughout Japan prayed for victory. The emperor commanded religious services day and night in all Shinto and Buddhist shrines and temples. Both he and the Retired Emperor wrote letters in their own hands beseeching the aid of the spirit world and sent them to the tombs of their ancestors. All Japan that was not fighting or preparing to fight was praying or chanting incantations to ensure victory.

The struggle lasted for more than 50 days. Accounts of it that have come down to us are so confused that it cannot be said which side had the upper hand. After the Japanese withstood the initial shock of the attack they probably gained a long-term advantage. Their armies were being constantly reinforced, and the Mongol invaders never penetrated far from the coast of Kyushu.

Whether or not the Mongols might ultimately have triumphed is an argument that will never be settled because nature—or the gods—took a decisive hand in the battle. Towards the end of August, as often happens in Japan at that season, dark clouds stood high in the south, and a great typhoon roared over Kyushu. For two days the wind blew at hurricane force. When the sky finally cleared, both enemy fleets were wrecked or scattered and most of their crews drowned. The demoralized invaders marooned on shore were quickly slaughtered by the Japanese.

The typhoon was the *kamikaze*, the "divine wind" whose timely intervention convinced the Japanese for many centuries to come that their land was specially protected by the gods. When another invasion threatened in the 20th century, the Japanese pilots who flew planes loaded with explosives into the guns of American warships in an effort to save their homeland were aptly named after the long-famed wind.

In repelling the Mongol conquerors, the Hojo regents achieved their greatest success. After that climax they were dogged by troubles that eventually grew unmanageable. For 20 years the Mongols threatened to mount another attack, and not until the death of Khubilai Khan in 1294 did the Japanese begin to feel secure. The war and the long alert had drained Japan economically and this strain on resources was to prove fatal to the *Bakufu* system of controlling the country.

Feudal loyalty compelled the important lords to obey the *Bakufu* orders and to call on their own vassals for services and supplies, but after similar commands before the Mongol invasion, the Hojo regents had rewarded their faithful supporters with land and other booty taken from opponents defeated in civil wars. No such rewards accrued from the defeat of the Mongols, and the *Bakufu* could not itself pay for military services since it had no funds—Japan had no nation-wide system of taxation. Most of the petitioners who now swarmed to Kamakura came away empty-handed, no matter how worthy their claims for recompense for wartime duties.

Grievances of disappointed claimants gradually weakened the bonds of loyalty that held the feudal system together. Great landholders, especially in distant parts of the country, began to behave more independently. Even when they became openly defiant, the *Bakufu* often could not make its other vassals act against them. Moreover, the waning strength of the *Bakufu* encouraged the Imperial Court to renew its plotting to regain real power. Its subtle intriguers found willing accomplices.

In 1318, following a long dispute about the imperial succession, an unusually vigorous emperor, Go Daigo, mounted the throne. Unlike some of his predecessors he was a full-grown man and fully resolved to restore the authority of the Imperial Family. The *Bakufu* tried repeatedly to force him to abdicate, but the Hojo regent at this time was weak-minded and debauched. Go Daigo was too much for him; for years he evaded the regent's orders, gaining supporters all the time.

In 1333 the Hojo leaders sent a powerful army to overawe the ambitious emperor, but its commanding general, Ashikaga Takauji, changed sides before he reached Kyoto and entered the capital in Go Daigo's name. His defection to the emperor signalled a wide revolt of discontented lords and their samurai, who marched on Kamakura and burned it to the ground. For a while it looked as if Go Daigo would actually succeed in restoring imperial power and, like the emperors of pre-feudal times, rule through ministers and provincial officials appointed by the Imperial Court. But his recently acquired general, Takauji, had personal ambitions. Backed by lords bent on maintaining their feudal powers, he managed to replace Go Daigo with a puppet emperor, and took over the Kyoto government as shogun. Go Daigo fled the capital and set up a rival Court in the mountains south of Kyoto.

The shogun of the line founded by Ashikaga Takauji were never as strong as Yoritomo or his Hojo-dominated successors, and within a century their power dwindled to almost nothing. For almost 300 years after Takauji's *coup d'état*, Japan seldom had an effective central government. The southern Court had been persuaded to return to Kyoto in 1392, but Japan's emperors remained shadows of the almost equally shadowy shogun. They gave only a trace of national unity while the nobleman of the provinces, the *daimyo* (great names), came to rule their fiefs like independent nations. A new stage of feudalism had begun.

挿鎗挟

A MAN OF WAR, *the armour-clad samurai personified the ideals of strength and courage of Japan's feudal age.*

THE WAY OF THE WARRIOR

The civil wars that swept Japan during the 12th century brought in a new age of strength and steel. Men from all over Japan joined the ranks of the warlike Taira and Minamoto clans in their battle for control of the country. A fierce new breed of armed noblemen, the samurai, began to emerge. Artisans turned their talents to the production of superb swords and armour, which combined beauty with a deadly practicality. Like the samurai shown above, in an illustration from a feudal manual on armour-wearing, Japan had put on the armour of war.

It took more than just a sword and a metal suit, however, to arm a samurai. Part of his equipment was moral and psychological—an austere, unwritten code of personal courage and loyalty roughly parallel to the rules of fealty in medieval Europe. The code, known as *bushido*, or "The Way of the Warrior", demanded an almost religious commitment to military life, in which physical hardship was the order of the day, and a heroic death in battle the most honourable goal.

UNDERPINNINGS: BASIC STEPS IN SELF-DEFENCE

A samurai's first duty was to die fighting for his lord. "If you think of saving your life," one legendary hero is supposed to have said, "you had better not go to war at all." Nevertheless, Japanese warriors still took the precaution of wearing elaborate, extremely effective armour in order to protect themselves from their opponents' swords.

The procedures for putting on the armour were complicated and time-consuming. The first steps, shown here, consisted of donning a series of undergarments: a special loincloth, a kimono of fine linen or brocade, and baggy trousers. These layers of cloth acted as padding over which the armour itself was strapped.

A warrior's next defence was his skill at fighting, acquired through years of rigorous training designed to build strength of character as well as physical prowess. Future samurai were apprenticed to masters of archery and swordsmanship, who toughened their bodies and spirits with extended fasts and barefoot treks through the snow. These hardships were to be endured without complaint, for as a character in a Japanese epic explains, if a man is a samurai, "when his stomach is empty, it is a disgrace to feel hungry".

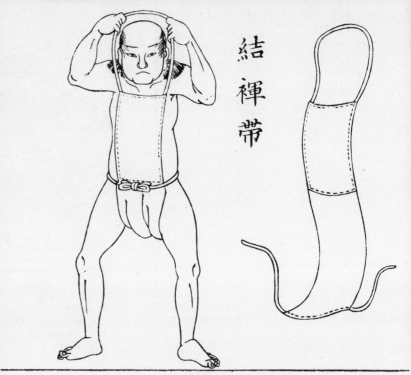

A COTTON BREECH-CLOUT *that extended up over the chest was the basic undergarment of a samurai's costume.*

A SHORT-SLEEVED KIMONO, *or "armour robe", was tied snugly at the waist with a special knot (lower right).*

服股衣

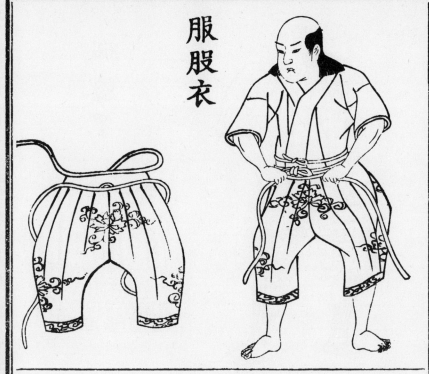

BILLOWING PANTALOONS, *worn over the armour robe, fitted loosely in the legs to allow freedom of movement.*

著臑當

STURDY SHINGUARDS *of cloth or leather were reinforced with strips of iron to give protection from the front.*

AN EXQUISITE BROCADE, *richly worked with a design of peonies, was one of the extravagant materials used in an armour robe that may have been made for a 14th-century imperial prince.*

A PLIABLE ARMOUR TO ABSORB THE SHOCKS

Despite the rigours of a samurai's training, his methods of combat were based on a principle of deftly applied "gentleness". The technique was similar to that of modern ju-jutsu (literally, "the gentle art"), in which an adroit flexibility of movement wins over brute strength.

The same principle applied to the construction of Japanese armour, which protected its wearer with flexibility and "give" instead of rigid bulk. Unlike European armour, with its massive steel plates, Japanese armour consisted of tiny scales of lacquered iron, or lamellae, laced together in rows with silk cords (*far right*). The result was a metallic fabric, as pliable as European chain mail, but considerably tougher.

Combined with flexibility, Japanese armour had the added advantage of being relatively light. While European knights were so encumbered by heavy steel that derricks were needed to lift them on to their horses, a samurai's armour weighed only about 25 pounds, allowing its wearer to leap with agility through rice paddies and over castle walls. In addition, it could be folded into a compact box for easy carrying when not in use, and if cut by a sword it could be mended by lacing on new lamellae.

DISPOSABLE THIGH GUARDS, *worn while on horseback, were often taken off for easy movement on foot.*

METAL-CASED SLEEVES *consisted of a Japanese type of chain mail and iron splints sewn on to heavy cloth.*

披身甲

A SHEATH FOR THE TORSO, *made from rows of iron lamellae, included armoured skirt-panels for the hips.*

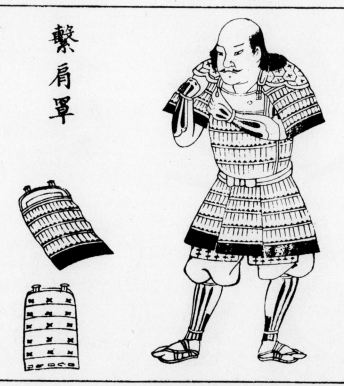

繋肩罩

BROAD SHOULDER GUARDS *of threaded lamellae hung like epaulets from the shoulders of the torso sheath.*

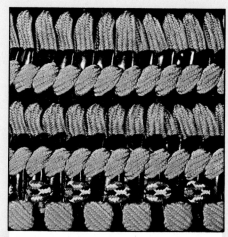

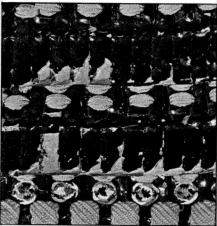

MULTICOLOURED STITCHING *of braided silk cord covered the outside surface (top) of Japanese armour. The cords held rows of lamellae, seen clearly from the armour's under side (bottom).*

HEADGEAR TO THWART AND TERRIFY THE FOE

In the man-to-man combat that characterized Japanese battles, samurai sometimes took as trophies the heads of their more important opponents. These they severed with the smaller of their two swords, carried specially for that purpose. This grisly custom prompted soldiers to wear particularly sturdy head-and-neck armour in order to avoid decapitation.

In addition to a helmet of riveted iron, warriors used special neck protectors and a metal face mask. The mask was usually shaped into a ferocious-looking countenance designed to intimidate the enemy. (Even before donning his mask, the samurai at the right has acquired an increasingly terrifying scowl.)

Despite their fierce aspect, warriors observed a strict set of courtesies before tangling with an adversary. Each combatant would announce his name, ancestry and previous deeds of heroism. When the fight was over, a victorious samurai would often compliment his defeated opponent on his bravery before taking his head. One courtesy extended past death itself; before a battle, a samurai burned incense in his helmet so that, if he were decapitated, his head would still smell sweet.

AN IRON COLLAR, *with a metal bib for additional protection, helped to guard its wearer against decapitation.*

A COTTON SKULL-CAP, *which helped to cushion the weight of the helmet, is tied over the warrior's head.*

蒙頰當

A GLOWERING MASK, *made of lacquered iron and strong enough to blunt a spear point, covered the face.*

IRON-RIB PROTECTION *for the head came from the riveted metal strips of this helmet. The neck fringe of stitched lamellae turns back at the side to reveal the warrior's family crest.*

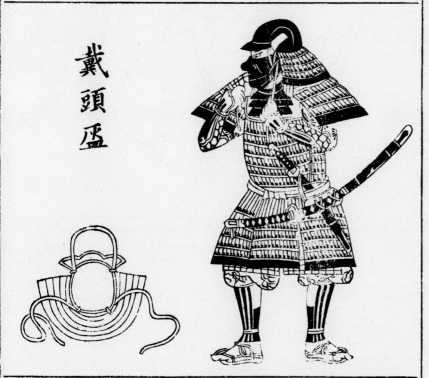

戴頭盔

A VISORED HELMET, *with an armoured fringe that guarded the back of the neck, completed the samurai's costume.*

A LIFELONG CONDITION OF COMBAT READINESS

Fighting was a samurai's life. He had to be ready at a moment's notice to answer a call to arms. Often he would have no time to fasten on his armour piece by piece, and he would be compelled to scramble into the whole ensemble all at once, by one of the emergency methods shown here.

Combat readiness extended beyond matters of equipment, and a good samurai was so thoroughly indoctrinated that he reacted instinctively to attack. A Japanese story tells of a young swordsman who apprenticed himself to a famous fencing master. One day, while cooking rice, he was given a painful whack with a wooden sword by his master. This treatment was repeated at unexpected hours of the day and night, until the youth learned never to relax his guard, and became the greatest swordsman in the land.

Once a samurai had mastered the techniques of his craft, he never let them drop. He trained daily, and often travelled about the country in search of ever-more-exacting teachers. His commitment to the art of war was total and unceasing, for according to his military code, "A samurai should live and die sword in hand. . . . To be brave and warlike must be his invariable condition".

UP FROM UNDER, *a samurai climbs quickly from below into a suit of armour that dangles from a hanger.*

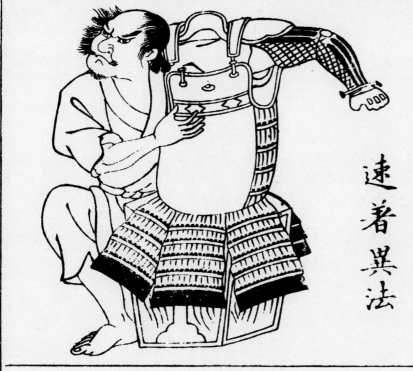

速著異法

IN FROM THE SIDE, *a warrior hurriedly slips into armour that has been pre-assembled on a special armour-stand.*

速被異法

A STRENUOUS TUSSLE *results when donning armour taken directly from its box—a method for emergencies only.*

A WARLORD'S SLEEVE, *this piece of engraved, gilded armour is believed to have been worn by a leader of the Minamoto clan, one of the principal military families of 12th-century Japan.*

4

MONKS AND MEN-AT-ARMS

Japan's early feudal age was born in violence, and it put hard-bitten provincial warriors in control of the country. But the age was nevertheless one of progress and change, and not a few of the traditions, attitudes and institutions that are characteristic of Japan today had their origins in the 12th and 13th centuries.

During the era known as the Kamakura period (1185–1333), when the Shogun Yoritomo and his Hojo successors ruled Japan from military headquarters at Kamakura, trade flourished and towns increased in number and size. Japanese artists and artisans improved the remarkable skills, especially sword-making, that would later win them fame all over the world. The samurai code of honour, later named *bushido*, began to develop from a simple set of loyalties into a powerful ethical code that is influential today. Buddhism, once supported mainly by nobles attracted by its aesthetic qualities, spread beyond the monasteries and became a national religion, producing several popular sects that are still important in Japan.

The bulk of Japan's people in the early feudal age were peasants, as in any simple agrarian society. Most of them were serfs bound to the land they cultivated and forced to surrender a large part of their crop to a landlord, usually a nobleman or a monastery. To these masses who tilled the soil, the comparative stability imposed by the early feudal rulers brought little change, but it had far-reaching consequences for the merchants and skilled artisans, whose numbers increased in Kamakura times. The coming and going between the imperial capital, Kyoto, and the shogun's headquarters at Kamakura, some 300 miles apart, stimulated travel and thereby opened new market areas to the merchant class. This led to the growth of commercial towns, which formed in much the same way as trading centres in medieval Europe. Settlements of merchants gathered at road junctions, at the gates of important monasteries, near the strongholds of noblemen who offered good protection and at natural harbours along the seacoast. The merchants attracted artisans and encouraged them to produce goods that could be sold, sent to other districts or shipped abroad.

A HEALING BUDDHA *holds a medicine pot in one hand and raises the other in blessing. As Buddhism became a popular religion in Japan in the 12th century, such Buddhas were venerated by lords and commoners alike.*

Until the Mongols conquered China, trade with the Chinese increased, and included such articles as delicate lacquerware, gracefully decorated fans and screens and finely wrought weapons. The fact that the finicky Chinese were eager to buy such goods was proof that Japanese taste and workmanship was catching up with China's.

In spite of the increasing importance of merchants and craftsmen, there was no doubt as to which class was the dominant one. It was the warriors, whose loyalty to their chiefs was the principal bond that held society together. The *élite* among these fighting men were the samurai—the mounted, armoured knights of aristocratic birth—but there were many accomplished fighters of lower status who had acquired good armour, weapons and even horses, perhaps by pillage or by robbing the bodies of slain warriors. It was also not uncommon for priests or monks of militant Buddhist sects to win fame on the field of battle.

The dominance of the warriors is vividly illustrated by the literature of Kamakura times, which was largely made up of vigorous stories about the exploits of fearless men-at-arms, and was very different from the delicate novels and poems of the Heian Age. No one knows who created the rousing Kamakura war tales. They were probably chanted to lute music by wandering minstrels and recounted in many versions before they were put on paper by monks or scholars. Unlike Heian literature, which was written by aristocrats for aristocrats, the Kamakura war stories were enormously popular with all classes, and the glorified warriors that they portray became national ideals of valour and honourable behaviour. Children with wooden swords re-enacted the heroes' mighty deeds. Artists painted their adventures on scrolls that were as popular as the tales themselves. This popularity still persists; the age of the crafty Yoritomo is Japan's heroic age.

The main subject of the war tales is the long, savage struggle for supremacy between the Taira and Minamoto families. The heroes are fabulous fighters, some of them from the ranks of the people, but glorified nevertheless. The language is wonderfully vivid, and great numbers of enemies are killed. A fine, loud example, from *The Tales of the Heike*, tells how a warrior-priest allied with the Minamoto fought his way across a bridge from which the planking had been removed:

> *[He] sprang forward alone on to the bridge and shouted in a mighty voice, "Let those at a distance listen; those that are near can see; I am Tsutsui Jomyo Meishu, the priest; who is there in Miidera who does not know me, a warrior worth one thousand men? Come on anyone who thinks himself someone, and we shall see!" And loosing off his 24 arrows like lightning flashes he slew 12 of the Heike [Taira] soldiers and wounded 11 more. . . . [He] cast off his footgear and springing barefoot on to the beams of the bridge he strode across. All were afraid to cross over, but he walked the broken bridge as one who walks along the street Ichijo or Nijo of the capital. With his "naginata" [pole sword] he mowed down five of the enemy, but with the sixth [it] snapped asunder . . . and flinging it away he drew his sword, wielding it in the zigzag style, the interlacing, cross, reversed dragonfly, water-wheel, and eight-sides-at-once styles of fencing, and cut down eight men.*

The heroes who fought such furious battles are described in full detail as they rode ahead of the army, disdaining strategy and tactics, to challenge an enemy champion in single combat. Gorgeous they were indeed:

> *Hon-sammi Chujo Shigehira . . . was attired that day in a [robe] of dark blue*

cloth on which a pattern of rocks and sea-birds was embroidered in light yellow silk, and armour with purple lacing deepening in its hue towards the skirts. On his head was a helmet with tall golden horns, and his sword also was mounted in gold. His arrows were feathered with black and white falcon plumes. . . . He was mounted on a renowned war-horse called Doji-kage, whose trappings were resplendent with ornaments of gold.

To modern readers of these gloriously bloody legends, a remarkable feature is the role played by women. Some of the champions in the war tales are girls, for in the early feudal age the women of Japan had not yet been reduced to the humble submissiveness that would be their posture in later centuries. They were expected to exhibit the same loyalty and bravery as the men, and occasionally a woman exceptionally endowed with these qualities won an honoured place in the warrior coterie. Tomoe of the Minamoto faction must have been such a one.

Tomoe had long black hair and a fair complexion, and her face was very lovely; moreover she was a fearless rider whom neither the fiercest horse nor the roughest ground could dismay, and so dexterously did she handle sword and bow that she was a match for a thousand warriors and fit to meet either god or devil. Many times had she taken field, armed at all points, and won matchless renown in encounters with the bravest captains, and so in this last fight, when all the others had been slain or had fled, among the last seven there rode Tomoe.

In spite of the great amount of fighting that they describe, the Kamakura war tales are not straightforward hero stories in which the good and the righteous win in the end. The opposite is true; the most attractive characters almost always lose and may even have their heads cut off as trophies. The commonest theme is the fall of the mighty from glory, and running through the scenes of battle and death is the basic Buddhist idea that life on earth is short, uncertain and full of sorrow and suffering.

The war tales were more than popular entertainment; they had a profound effect in shaping the modern Japanese character. By idealizing the hardihood, loyalty, self-sacrifice and contempt for death of the feudal heroes, they helped to establish the spartan and uncompromising samurai tradition that lasted for many centuries. In World War II the Japanese soldiers and civilians who killed themselves rather than endure the dishonour of surrender were 20th-century products of the heroic tales first chanted by the minstrels of the Kamakura Age.

The material symbol of the martial spirit of the times was the warrior's principal weapon, his sword. In later years the privilege of carrying this deadly, razor-sharp blade came to be reserved for the knightly samurai, but during the Kamakura period some men of lower birth also had swords and used them to carve their way to glory. A sword was not, however, a weapon only; to the samurai especially it was the central object of an elaborate cult of honour. For a samurai to be parted from his sword was to lose his honour. Samurai were accustomed to sleeping with their swords beside their pillows; when a young samurai was about to be born, a sword was brought into the room, and when a samurai died his sword was placed beside his death-bed.

Swords were thought to have miraculous powers and lives of their own. Soldiers defeated in battle prayed at the shrines of the war-god Hachiman, asking why their swords had lost their spirit. Many stories have come down about the spiritual powers of notable blades. One of these tells about two famous swordsmiths, named Muramasa and Masamune, who were almost equal in skill. When a sword made by Muramasa was held upright in a running stream, every dead leaf that drifted against the edge was cut neatly in two. This was a good performance, but not the best. When a Masamune sword was put to the same test, the floating leaves avoided its edge and passed unhurt on either side; Masamune's blade therefore possessed spiritual power over the leaves and was superior to its rival.

Because of the importance of swords and the mystical significance attached to them, the sword-makers were an honoured class, and they approached their task with great solemnity. Before forging their blades they underwent fasting and ritual purification, and they worked at their anvils and forges in white clothes like the robes of priests. Their efforts were well rewarded; as early as the 13th century, Japanese swords were far superior to any made elsewhere in the world. Not until the development of modern scientific metallurgy in the 19th century could Europeans make steel approaching 13th-century Japanese steel in quality, or even understand how the Japanese did it.

To produce their superlative blades, Japanese artisans had to resolve a stubborn dilemma that has confronted all armourers since earliest times. They could make steel very hard so that it would hold a sharp edge through violent use in battle, but swords made from it would be apt to break because such steel is brittle. They could also make soft steel that would not break, but the edge then could not be made as keen, and it dulled quickly in use. It could not hack through armour and do the other things, such as lopping off arms and heads, that a proper sword is expected to do.

One way in which the Japanese swordsmiths solved this problem closely resembled the method used by the Saracen steelmakers of Damascus and the Spaniards who made Toledo blades famous. Layers of steel of varying hardness were hammered together to weld them into a metal sandwich. The sandwich was then reheated, folded back on itself and hammered out thin again. After this had been repeated about a dozen times, the steel consisted of thousands of paper-thin laminations of hard and soft metal. When it was ground to a sharp edge, the hard steel stood out and resisted dulling while the soft steel kept the blade from snapping.

But to produce their best blades, the Japanese used a much more intricate process. For the core, or interior, of such a blade, they used comparatively soft, laminated metal that would resist breaking. The blade's exterior and edge, however, were made of different grades of hard steels welded together into a sandwich that was folded and hammered out as many as 20 times, giving it more than a million laminations. This outer "skin" of steel could be made even harder by heating and sudden cooling. As a final step the master smith carefully covered the roughly finished blade with a thick layer of adhesive material, mostly clay, leaving only the edge exposed, and heated it to the proper temperature, until the glowing metal reached the right shade of colour. The best way to judge this crucially delicate stage was to work at dawn in a darkened room. Then, with prayer, the smith plunged the blade in water. The exposed edge cooled instantly and became extremely hard, but the rest of the blade, protected by the clay, cooled slowly and remained comparatively soft. The final result was a sword blade of soft, non-brittle metal enclosed in a thin layer of hard steel. About one-fifth of an inch of its edge was made of metal so hard that it held its razor sharpness during repeated use in battle.

These marvellous blades were fitted with long hilts so that they could be wielded with both hands, and cutting off human heads was easy for them. So common was this conclusive stroke that warriors sometimes wore steel anti-decapitation collars to prolong their careers, but a really good sword could hew through armour and even cut a man in two at a single blow.

The most admired swords were those that had been tested repeatedly in battle. They were heirlooms passed down in samurai families for many generations and were not plentiful. Many a young samurai was forced to accept a newly forged sword without a pedigree, and he was naturally eager to know its worth. He, or the sword-maker himself, might first try the blade on bundles of straw simulating human flesh. If a sword qualified, it was tested on a human corpse that might be suspended in various positions to permit different cutting strokes. Sometimes a sword was tried on a criminal condemned to death. One story tells of a burly robber who sat in the stocks awaiting execution. When the swordsman walked up with a naked blade he asked: "Is it you who will cut me down?"

"Yes," was the reply.... "I shall cut you in the *kesa* [shoulder to side] style...."

"If I had known it before," said the robber, "I would have swallowed a couple of big stones to spoil your sword."

Along with the glorification of the warrior in Kamakura times came a religious awakening that began to sweep Japan towards the end of the 12th century. Dissenters broke away from orthodox Buddhist doctrines and practices, and many new and popular sects were founded. Some of them were "redemptionist", offering hope of paradise in the life to come. One sect adapted its philosophical principles to the warrior's spartan traditions and his cult of the sword, and another

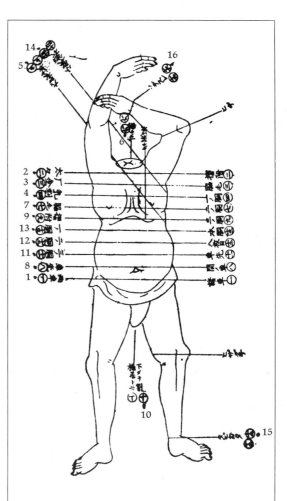

TESTS FOR NEW SWORDS

Before accepting a new sword, a samurai had its blade extensively tested—often on the body of a beheaded criminal (*above*). Cuts, which had exotic names, varied in difficulty from one across the hips (1), the hardest, to lopping off a hand (16).

1 ryo kuruma—"*pair of wheels*"
2 tai-tai—"*very big*"
3 karigane—"*wild goose*"
4 chiwari—"*splitting the breast*"
5 o-kesa—"*priest's robe*"
6 kami-tatewari—"*top vertical split*"
7 wakige—"*armpit*"
8 kurumasaki—"*end of the wheel*"
9 suritsuke—"*rubbing in*"
10 shimo-tatewari—"*bottom vertical split*"
11 san-no-do—"*third body cut*"
12 ni-no-do—"*second body cut*"
13 ichi-no-do—"*first body cut*"
14 ko-kesa—"*small priest's robe*"
15 tabigata—"*sock region*"
16 sodesuri—"*cutting the sleeve*"

sometimes resorted to the sword to spread its faith throughout the country.

All these numerous sects broadened the appeal of a religion that at first drew adherents mainly from the upper classes. Soon after Buddhism arrived in Japan from China and Korea in the sixth century, it became an established Church supported by the Court and the ruling nobility, who appreciated the gorgeous rituals, impressive literature and artistic objects associated with it. As the centuries passed, its temples and monasteries grew enormously rich from gifts and legacies, and some of them became corrupt and more concerned with wealth and ostentation than with the fasts, prayers, readings and other austerities that their doctrines held to be important. They were often oppressors of the people who lived on the rich lands that they owned, and they were consequently hated.

The early Japanese types of Buddhism were further handicapped as popular religions by their insistence on the evil and vanity of all worldly life. For men who were willing to desert their families, become monks and withdraw from the world, such an attitude was not unattractive, but for the ordinary man, with his much-loved family, his home, his hopes and his troubles, this lofty, ascetic kind of Buddhism had little appeal as a guide to life. During most of the Heian Age the typical Japanese probably held such Buddhist beliefs as reincarnation and karma, the doctrine that a man's present life is controlled by his behaviour in previous lives. That was about all. These basic beliefs, generously mixed with primitive superstition, were the chief contribution of early Buddhism to the spiritual life of the general population.

But Buddhism was not a single religion. For many centuries before it reached Japan it had been a family of numerous religions, and some of its divisions and sects were not all monkish or

withdrawn. Even in India, where Buddhism was born in about the sixth century B.C. and where it taught that all life was pain and suffering, sects had developed that saw the Buddha as a joyous saviour bringing hope and happiness to the earth. This is how the Mahavastu, an Indian sacred scripture, describes a visit of the Buddha: "As he came into the city ... all unsightly rocks, gravel and pebbles disappeared into the earth, leaving it covered with masses of flowers. Flowering trees blossomed; fruit-bearing trees bore fruit. ... The blind saw; the deaf heard. The insane recovered their reason; the sick were healed, and women with child were safely delivered. The naked appeared clad, and the fetters of those in bondage were loosened".

Indeed there was cheer in Buddhism for those who would see it, and after a thousand years some of it reached Japan via China, in the form of the worship of Amida, one of the innumerable gods that the old, many-sided faith had acquired. Amida, the Lord of Boundless Light, was believed to have been an Indian prince who earned enlightenment by arduous devotions and established a paradise, the Pure Land," thousands of millions of leagues in the west", where he welcomed pious believers who invoked his name.

At first Amida was worshipped in Japan as merely one of many gods and godlike beings, and devotees in the monasteries were accustomed to watch the sunset while meditating about the glories of his western paradise. Later, as the golden Heian Age sank into decay and pessimism and disorder increased, the news of Amida's welcoming paradise began to spread. A leader of this movement was a monk named Genshin, author of a book, *The Essentials of Salvation*, that taught that the best way for a person to be reborn in the Pure Land was to repeat piously *"Namu Amida Butsu"*, a phrase that was called the *nembutsu* and meant "homage to Amida Buddha". When such a devoted person dies, wrote Genshin, "the Lord of Compassion brings a lotus flower to carry the pious soul, and the Lord of Might reaches him welcoming hands. . . . Born in the Land of Purity, the pious man is like a blind man who suddenly recovers his sight and finds himself surrounded by radiant beams and brilliant jewels of untold price. . . . Some of the beings in paradise are singing in adoration of Buddha . . . while others are poised in the air in serene meditation. Amida Buddha sits on a lotus seat like a golden mountain . . . surrounded by his saints. The Lords of Compassion and of Might lead the newly born before the Buddha's seat".

Genshin was an inspired prophet but an indifferent proselytizer. Not until long after his death in 1017 did his glorious vision of Amidism really take hold outside the monasteries. In 1175 a monk named Honen formed the *Jodo*, or Pure Land, sect and began preaching that the power of the *nembutsu* is absolute and universal. It could be used by people of any class and any condition, even by the worst of sinners, and if they were sincere, it would surely win them admission into the Pure Land. This was great good news in a war-troubled age. Many people were convinced that the dark "latter days of the law", long predicted by Buddhist sages, had come indeed, and that man was too degenerate to depend on his own spiritual powers. It was therefore proper to appeal to the power of another, such as Amida.

Bringing consolation and hope of rebirth in paradise, the Pure Land sect spread rapidly among all classes, the high as well as the low. One Retired Emperor during the Kamakura period is reported to have repeated the *nembutsu* several million times and to have died while reciting it. Even fierce samurai joined the sect. Some of them, apparently tired of a warrior's life, killed themselves in the belief that the *nembutsu* would gain them rebirth in Amida's delightful paradise.

One of Honen's followers, Shinran, taught that even a single sincere invocation of Amida's name was sufficient. Once a person was thus assured of reaching the western paradise, further repetitions were unnecessary. There was no need for him to live as a monk, indulge in austerities or follow religious rules. He could marry, have children and enjoy life on earth without jeopardizing his salvation. Shinran himself married and had six children, and the priests of his sect, which is still strong, are usually married men today.

Some scholars have seen in such "salvation" sects as the Amidists, a striking parallel to the Protestant sects of Europe's Reformation. Both taught salvation by faith instead of by "works", such as giving property to the Church, or obeying religious rules. Scriptural authority for salvation by faith is found in the Apostle Paul's declaration, "For whosoever shall call upon the name of the Lord shall be saved" (Romans 10.13), which is remarkably like Honen's recommendation of the *nembutsu*. Other resemblances between Protestantism and the Buddhist salvation sects were their married clergy, the revivalist fervour that they shared, and the tendency in both towards a Church governed by independent congregations instead of by high prelates.

The popularity of the Amidists enraged the older Buddhist sects, who did what they could to suppress their new rivals. The Emperor Go Toba threw his weight against the Amida sects. Some of Honen's disciples were exiled to wild northern Japan, others beheaded. In 1207 Honen himself was sent into exile for four years, but was allowed to return to Kyoto a short time before he died. When he was on his death-bed, his followers brought a small image of Amida and, as was their custom, tied one end of a cord to its hand

and offered the other end to Honen so that the Buddha could lead him into paradise. Honen refused. Already, he said, he saw in the sky a great crowd of Buddhas waiting to welcome him into the Pure Land.

Honen and Shinran, as well as most of their followers, were tolerant and benign, but a later reformer monk, Nichiren, was intolerant and aggressive. The violent religion that he founded, the *Hokke*, or Lotus, sect, had little resemblance to other kinds of Buddhism. Nichiren believed that the other Buddhist sects were spoiling the Japanese national vigour and corrupting the country's secular rulers. He taught that truth lies only in the Lotus Sutra, an ancient Buddhist scripture written in India, and that the only way for a person to enter paradise is by repeating the formula *"Namu-myoho-renge-kyo"* (homage to the wonderful law of the Lotus Sutra). Whoever neglects to do this, Nichiren said, will go to a luridly flaming hell, and any recognition of other kinds of Buddhism will land him in hell also. Nichiren attacked all sects, denouncing their leaders as liars, thieves, hypocrites, fiends, devils and brigands. Naturally he met opposition; he was repeatedly persecuted and twice exiled. On one occasion he was about to be executed but, according to his account, "a bright object like a ball of fire" blazed across the sky and so frightened the executioner that he could not use his sword.

Tirelessly the furious monk foretold all sorts of disasters if his teachings were not followed to the exclusion of all others. In 1260 and 1268 he predicted a foreign invasion, something that Japan had not suffered in its recorded history. When the Mongols did attack in 1274 and again in 1281, he claimed credit for miraculous foresight and won many samurai to his militant sect.

Like many another prophet, Nichiren identified his doctrines with the well-being of the State. He claimed that Japan could not thrive unless he were accepted as its religious leader. He even planned to found a world-conquering religion with its Holy See in Japan.

Nichiren's followers became even more violent than he. They armed themselves and roamed the country burning the buildings of rival sects. Monasteries and temples had been burned before, but the armed monks so plentiful in earlier Japanese history had fought for power, property and privilege; Nichiren's Lotus sect was the first to use religion as a motive for its militancy. Its claim to be identified with the country's welfare was later interpreted as desirable patriotism, and the sect has been popular in modern times among extreme nationalists. Shortly before World War II, when the militarists were taking over the Japanese government, their cause was aided by a programme of terror carried out by fanatical assassins who were members of the Lotus sect. It is active today and still possesses a flavour of super-patriotism.

Strikingly different from other kinds of Buddhism was Zen, a mystical sect that reached Japan from China and won great influence with the Kamakura military rulers because of its emphasis on discipline and austerity. Zen (the word is derived from Sanskrit and means "meditation") was supposed to have been founded in India by a monk named Bodhidharma, who sat and stared at a blank wall for nine years. Such admiration of extreme asceticism is typically Indian, and Zen has some other Indian traits, but it was mostly a Chinese creation that, like other things Chinese, reached its highest development in Japan.

The central idea of Zen is sudden enlightenment, a recognition of the illusory nature of all existence. Enlightenment was held to be beyond all price, more valuable than any teaching and compared by some to direct communication with the soul of the Buddha. Most other kinds of Buddhism taught that enlightenment must be earned painfully by study, prayer and holy living, and that it usually comes as the climax of many lives of reincarnation. Zen taught that enlightenment may come in a flash as the result of intense mental and physical discipline. During this effort the mind is not supposed to be thinking in the ordinary sense. Instead, it concentrates on problems, called *koan*, that are derived from the sayings of Zen masters. These problems are deliberately illogical or even absurd. Perhaps the most famous of them is "When both hands are clapped, a sound is produced; listen to the sound of one hand". The proper handling of this *koan* had nothing to do with sound waves, air currents or anything else rational. It was meant to be wholly irrational and was intended to put a strain on the mind and bring it to the brink of sudden enlightenment. The Zen master often helped to jolt the disciple's mind into enlightenment by shouting in his ear ("*Ho!*" in China, "*Katsu!*" in Japan), or beating him with a stick.

A monk named Eisai is sometimes considered the founder of Japanese Zen, but the more influential pioneer was an aristocrat named Dogen (1200-1253), who modified Chinese Zen to fit the temperament of Japan's military governing class.

Dogen was a high-ranking nobleman of the Imperial Court but on his return from China, where he attained enlightenment, he avoided both the Imperial Court at Kyoto and the shogun's capital at Kamakura. He spent most of his life in secluded monasteries where he guided his disciples towards sudden enlightenment.

His methods were drastic and based on *zazen* (literally "sitting in meditation"): a special kind of meditation in a cross-legged position. This position, maintained for many hours, was intended to allay the passions of anger, vexation and selfishness while composing and emptying the mind. In one of his treatises Dogen wrote: "Free yourself from all attachments and bring to rest the 10,000 things. Think neither good nor evil and judge not right nor wrong. Maintain the flow of the mind, of will and of consciousness; bring to an end all desires, all concepts and judgements. . . . The body must be maintained upright. . . . Ears and shoulders, nose and navel must be kept in alignment respectively. The tongue is to be kept against the palate, lips and teeth are kept firmly closed, while the eyes are to be kept always open".

Dogen's disciples held to a strict and rigorous régime. For breakfast and supper they got a small amount of rice, and lunch was no doubt equally frugal. Every day for long periods they sat in silent, motionless *zazen*. If they drowsed, the Zen master woke them up with his ready stick. Sleep was permitted for only six hours or so each night, and it was broken by several short stints of *zazen*. The reward might be enlightenment.

Zen made few converts among the common people but had a powerful appeal to the dominant warriors of Kamakura times. Several shogun and their regents became Zen converts. These hardy soldier-aristocrats had passed through rigorous physical and moral training, and it was only natural for them to applaud the discipline required of Zen devotees. They also made a fetish of strict obedience, on which the structure of feudal society depended, and therefore they admired the way that Zen disciples obeyed every word of the Zen masters. Another quality of Zen that delighted the often illiterate warriors was its anti-intellectualism. Dogen himself was a learned man, who urged his followers to read the Buddhist Sutras, but other Zen masters made much of scoffing at bookish knowledge and rejecting logic and other mental skills. All that was needed, they said, was discipline and fortitude, and of course the guidance of a good Zen master.

The soldiers, who were the principal patrons of Zen, seem to have had a strong influence on the sect. Although Zen is a kind of Buddhism and therefore ostensibly opposed to all shedding of blood, Zen masters quickly became the leading elaborators of Japan's ancient cult of the sword.

Zen masters, however, did not themselves teach the physical details of fencing; instead they laid their stress on correct moral attitude. According to one Zen master writing about A.D. 1600, a really good Zen swordsman must free his consciousness of all thought of death while in combat. Then he will not watch his opponent's sword. Such action would be fatal, for his mind would stop for an instant and permit his opponent to deal a deadly blow. Instead, he must ignore his opponent's death-dealing efforts. Once his mind is fluid and free of all "stops", his sword will become fully alive and give him the victory.

Some Zen masters must have had uncomfortable Buddhist feelings of guilt about the bloodshed associated with swordsmanship. At least, the literature of Zen contains some remarkable rationalizations. Says D. T. Suzuki, a leading modern expounder of Zen: "The sword is generally associated with killing, and most of us wonder how it can come into connection with Zen, which is a

school of Buddhism teaching the gospel of love and mercy. The fact is that the art of swordsmanship distinguishes between the sword that kills and the sword that gives life. The one that is used by a technician cannot go any further than killing, for he never appeals to the sword unless he intends to kill. The case is altogether different with the one who is compelled to lift the sword. For it is really not he but the sword itself that does the killing. He has no desire to do harm to anybody, but the enemy appears and makes himself a victim. It is as though the sword performs automatically its function of justice, which is the function of mercy. . . . When the sword is expected to play this sort of role in human life, it is no more a weapon of self-defence or an instrument of killing".

Zen was, and still is, an extraordinarily adaptable sect. As soon as it became powerful in 13th and 14th-century Japan, it began branching out in many directions, eventually touching and influencing most sectors of Japanese cultural life. The early Zen temples of the Kamakura period were as plain and austere as Zen principles, but soon they began to grow more elaborate, probably due to the sect's popularity among the wealthy ruling class. Zen temples also became important patrons of the arts. Besides sponsoring contests in wrestling, fencing and archery to please their simpler soldier patrons, they also encouraged poetry, painting, calligraphy and flower-arranging— that charming and most Japanese artistic activity. They gave special attention to the art of gardening, and many celebrated Japanese gardens with their carefully positioned stones, pools and banks of moss are Zen creations. In an era dominated by warriors, Zen's support to artists and intellectuals laid the foundation for a renaissance that would in the following age carry Japan's cultural achievements to a new level of brilliance.

Deliberately stark, islands of rock rise out of a calm sea of sand in the garden of the Zen Buddhist Ryoanji Temple in Kyoto.

THE WORLD IN A GARDEN

The ancient gardens in and around Kyoto are among the foremost creations of Oriental art. And yet they were designed not so much to produce aesthetic pleasure as to promote a meditative calm. Contemplation of man's place in the cosmos plays an essential part in Zen, a Buddhist sect that became Japan's most influential religion in the 13th century; accordingly, the gardens that Zen priests and laymen studied during their meditations were symbolic, miniature versions of the world of nature. The profundity of nature could best be rendered, Zen gardeners thought, not by ornate statues and brightly coloured trees, but by evergreens, dark mosses and rustic paths, or by a stark design of black rocks on white sand. Such gardens, they believed, preserved some of the mystery and the spirit of a lesson taught by the Buddha who, when asked to define ultimate reality, silently pointed to a flower.

A flat cone of sand, designed to appear in moonlight as a study in white, gleams in the garden of the Silver Pavilion in Kyoto.

In the solemn beauty of sand against foliage, gardens that were inspired by Zen ink paintings

One of the strongest influences exerted on Zen gardening was ink painting, and many sand gardens were attemps to translate two-dimensional pictures into three-dimensional landscapes. Ink painting, or "sumi-e", was a highly suggestive and deceptively simple technique; with only a few strokes of black ink on white silk the artist could evoke a mountain lost in mist or a bottomless ravine. Several of the leading Zen painters were also gardeners who duplicated their monochromatic paintings in natural materials, employing sand to represent the silk, and dark stones and greenery to stand for the brushwork. Like the paintings, these gardens were kept simple; as one 16th-century painter-gardener wrote, "Caution should be taken not to be too anxious to overcrowd the scenery to make it more interesting. Such an effect often results in a loss of dignity and a feeling of vulgarity".

Clipped azalea bushes border a 17th-century sand garden near Kyoto and suggest mountains seen across an expanse of water.

The hidden symbolism
of a sacred grove

*Although Kyoto's Saihoji garden
looks at first glance like a beautiful
segment of untutored nature, it was
actually planned with infinite care.
A pond was dug around two islands
to form the Japanese character
meaning "heart" or "soul", a key
Zen term that denotes an unself-
conscious spontaneity considered
very desirable. Maples were planted
so that their autumn colours would
brighten the shadowy grove, and
more than 50 different varieties of
moss were cultivated to cover the
ground with a velvety carpet. So
luxuriant did Saihoji become that
legends claimed it was the sacred
precinct of beneficent spirits.*

The tea-house garden— a retreat from the world

During the 15th and 16th centuries Japan was constantly torn by internal wars. The men of this period, however, found a refuge from constant strife in the tea ceremony, a ritual of elegant simplicity that developed in this period.

Essentially, the tea ceremony was nothing more than a gathering of a few friends in a small house, set in a secluded garden; the purpose in meeting was to drink tea and discuss a work of art—often a utensil used in making and serving the tea.

The tea-house garden was laid out to a prescribed plan. An entrance path (left) led to the outer garden and a small shelter where guests gathered. After the tea-master arrived, the guests proceeded into an inner garden. There they performed ritual purification by rinsing their hands and mouths in a basin (above, right) before entering the low door of the tea-house (below, right).

Every detail of the tea-garden had to have the correct natural charm, which one tea-master, Rikyu, understood better than anyone else how to achieve. Once, after he had ordered his son to sweep a path twice until it was spotlessly clean, Rikyu shook a branch and carefully littered the neat stones with leaves.

A flagstone path leads to the entrance of Ura-Senke, a Kyoto tea-garden.

A dipper lies across a water basin at Ura-Senke. Originally, such basins were situated near temples for the ablutions of worshippers.

The door to a tea-house at Ura-Senke is so low that guests must kneel to enter; such a doorway is called "a humble entrance".

A priest's study and a garden to refresh the spirit

Gardens played such a vital role in the meditations of Zen monks that their residences were often planned as little more than a frame for the view. The uncomplicated interior of this part of the 16th-century Daisenin monastery in Kyoto led the eye irresistibly to a carefully designed landscape of rugged stones, raked gravel and trees outside. Within the confining area of only a few square yards, the gardener constructed a dry facsimile of a watery paradise. A small bridge and an adjoining wall in the centre of the picture spanned a stream of gravel; to the left of the bridge, stones were placed to represent waterfalls, dams and islands.

Scenic wonders for
aristocratic excursions

As the influence of Zen gardening
spread throughout Japanese culture,
its precepts were adopted—and
sometimes ridiculously exaggerated—
by wealthy dilettantes. In Zen
temples and monasteries, gardens
were small, symbolic and designed to
be looked at from one viewpoint. On
many private estates, however, huge
tracts of land, like the Jojuen garden
shown on the right, were turned into
parks for strolling; here the emphasis
was not on religious meditation but
upon secular amusement. Miniature
artificial hills resembling Mount Fuji
were created, as well as replicas of
famous beaches and rivers.

Nobles and samurai vied with one
another in paying fabulous sums for
unusual rocks, in employing
thousands of people to transplant
pines, and in building scores of
bridges, verandas and tiny pavilions
for the viewing of cherry blossoms.
Expeditions for looking at the
blooming cherry trees were such a
craze that one poet, holding fast to
the Zen notion that true beauty lay in
the more subdued aspects of nature,
wrote: "To those who only pray for
the cherries to bloom/How I wish to
show the spring/That gleams from a
patch of green/In the midst of the
snow-covered mountain-village".

5

THE COUNTRY
AT WAR

In the 14th century the military dictatorship that controlled Japan was seized by new rulers, the Ashikaga clan. Politically, their régime was a disaster. They were unable to keep a rein on the fractious provincial barons, nor could they prevent the country from breaking up into more then 60 principalities, each semi-independent and each mainly preoccupied with warring on its neighbours. And yet, in the midst of this bloodshed and anarchy, Japan prospered. The Ashikaga inaugurated a period of memorable glory, when population and wealth increased, the arts shone as never before, and for the first time in their history the Japanese people made themselves felt far from their sheltered islands. By the close of the 15th century, Japanese sea traders—pirates more often than not—had extended Japanese influence over East Asian seas and shores. The island nation, though hopelessly divided, was rich and cultured, ready to bedazzle its first European visitors.

Both the successes and the failures of the Ashikaga shogunate were affected by a seemingly minor matter of geography. The Ashikaga made their main headquarters in the ancient capital of Kyoto. When Japan's first shogun, Yoritomo, had assumed power late in the 12th century, he deliberately avoided Kyoto for fear that his warriors would be corrupted by the subtle aristocrats of the Imperial Court. He as well as his immediate successors felt that Kamakura was a healthier place for the apex of the feudal pyramid. But the Ashikaga shogun had no taste for life in the crude, rough eastern provinces. Though they maintained a branch headquarters at Kamakura, they spent most of their time in magnificent palaces that they built in a section of Kyoto known as the Muromachi quarter. The result was just what Yoritomo would have predicted: a softening of the shogunate's officers by association with the aristocratic Court.

There was another result as well that Yoritomo might not have predicted, or cared much about. The part of the Japanese capital where the Ashikaga shogun set themselves up in great luxury gave its name to a time in the 15th and 16th centuries known as the Muromachi period, when Japan's art and culture reached a glorious high point.

At first the provincial nobles of the Ashikaga faction who came to live in Kyoto acted like *nouveaux riches*, contemptuous of a higher culture but still attracted to it. Stories survive of the insults they and their retainers offered to the poverty-stricken exquisites of the metropolis, and even to the powerless Imperial Family. On one occasion, for example, a Retired Emperor (called an *In* in Japanese) was rudely addressed on the streets of the capital by a drunken and insolent warrior. When a member of the royal retinue reproved him, the soldier cried, "What is this *In* you speak of? If you mean an *Inu* [dog], I'll shoot it!" Then the warrior and his followers shot arrows at the *In's* carriage and cut the harness of the oxen so that the animals ran away. The Retired Emperor was left standing in the street, his eyes filled with tears at the indignity he had suffered.

This period of tension did not last long. The Ashikaga supporters were soon making friends as best they could with Kyoto's aloof aristocrats, imitating their elaborate courtesies and employing them as the equivalent of modern social secretaries. Some of the provincial barons married into ancient families. During the time of the most notable of the Ashikaga, Yoshimitsu, who was shogun from 1367 to 1394 and then ruled from retirement until his death in 1408, many of the most powerful families in Japan had moved to the capital, built mansions there and were competing with Yoshimitsu in cultivating the arts and practising good manners.

With this infusion of power and wealth the old city revived, attracted artists and intellectuals, and paid them well. A leading role in this renaissance was played by Zen Buddhism, which had become the leading upper-class religion in early feudal times and was now stronger than

ever. Its centres had grown from humble hermitages to imposing buildings with sweeping curved tile roofs, and Zen monks and priests were no longer recluses devoted to silence and meditation. They entered the service of the new military rulers and made themselves political advisers, diplomats and legal and financial experts. They perfected a new system of bookkeeping to ensure the proper investment of their temples' large funds. They ran Japan's leading college, which taught Chinese philosophy and other classical Chinese studies, and set up an elaborate system of schools to instruct young people in reading and writing and moral behaviour.

Much the same was also done by the Christian clerics of Europe's Middle Ages and for the same reason, to compensate for the ignorance of the feudal aristocracy. But Zen clerics went even further by financing and organizing Japan's foreign trade. Yoshimitsu was an extravagant shogun, and his costly art collections and reckless building of palaces, temples and monasteries ran up debts that the government's tax revenues and the income from his family estates could not cover. The astute Zen monks had a solution for this deficit: the profits to be made from officially stimulated trade with China, the source of many luxuries for which wealthy Japanese were willing to pay heavily.

The monks were no new-comers to the field of commerce. As early as 1342, taking advantage of the first stirrings of Chinese rebellion against Mongol oppression, they had sponsored a ship for the China trade; its profits were expected to endow a temple. Thereafter the traffic grew slowly, with many temples and monasteries, as well as feudal lords in south-western Japan, taking a hand. The ships generally carried presents for the Ming emperor. The self-centred Chinese considered the gifts a kind of tribute, but the Japanese did not

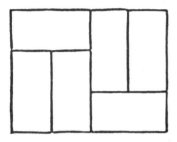

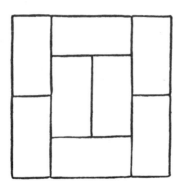

FLOOR MATS, *or "tatami", were an integral part of house design in the aristocratic mansions of 15th-century Kyoto. Each mat measured about three feet by six, and the size of a room was determined according to the number of mats it was to contain. Small rooms commonly had six mats (above) or eight mats (right). The mats were arranged in decorative patterns, which in larger designs resembled tightly coiled spirals (below).*

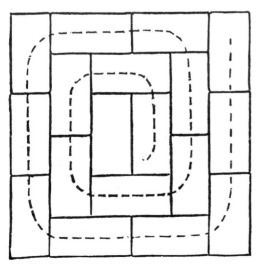

object outwardly to this implication because the presents that the Chinese sent in return were usually far more valuable than the "tribute" they had received.

The Chinese were not much interested in trade with the Japanese, or with anyone, for its own sake, but they were interested in getting rid of the Japanese pirates who had been raiding their northern coasts, and they were willing to grant concessions to end the harassment. They approached Yoshimitsu, the first of the Ashikaga line with effective power in western Japan, and soon he was exchanging letters with the Chinese Court through his Zen advisers. In A.D. 1402 the negotiations with China produced definite results. Yoshimitsu, by then ruling from retirement, agreed to suppress the pirates in exchange for lucrative trade. His forces vigorously attacked the pirate bases on the islands of Iki and Tsushima in the Korea straits and forwarded a batch of captives to China. Officials of the Chinese emperor returned them with thanks to the Japanese, who boiled them alive. According to a contemporary Chinese account, the large copper kettle in which the punishment was carried out was exhibited as a warning to pirates still unboiled.

After this cordial exchange, trade with China went briskly, protected by both countries but organized in Japan by monk-financiers who commissioned merchants from coastal cities to handle the physical details. The principal articles imported from China were raw silk, brocades, porcelains and Chinese copper coins, which were used as currency in Japan in Ashikaga times. The Japanese paid for these goods with sulphur from their volcanic islands and with their wonderful swords. Objects of art moved in both directions. The Japanese sent fans and decorated screens, their specialities, while the Chinese sent books and paintings. To the monks, the cultural exchange represented by these articles may have seemed as important as the financial profits.

The trade with China, particularly the influx of Chinese coinage, gave the western parts of Japan a hectic prosperity. Many seaport towns increased in size and wealth, and a prosperous merchant class clustered around their harbours. The most important was Sakai, today a port near the great industrial centre of Osaka. Its rich merchants issued bills of exchange somewhat similar to modern cheques, engaged armed fleets to guard their shipping, and lent money to thriftless aristocrats, one of the neediest of whom was Ashikaga Yoshimitsu himself. While he was shogun, he had lavished enormous sums on the Palace of Flowers, his elegant residence in the Muromachi quarter of Kyoto. For his retirement in 1394, he had built a splendid monastery, part of which was the famous Golden Pavilion, an elaborate gilded building that combined living quarters, entertainment halls and a chamber for quiet meditation.

The later Ashikaga shogun were hardly less profligate than Yoshimitsu but not so strong; as they grew progressively feebler the country broke up in many different ways. More and more daimyo felt strong enough to challenge the shogunate, ruling their domains as virtually independent territories, and local wars of conquest became common. In weakly ruled provinces secondary vassals defied their overlords and were defied in turn by their own vassals. Guilds of merchants fortified their towns and enlisted soldiers to protect their shipments from bandits. Some daimyo kept reasonable order in their fiefs, but elsewhere even the peasants revolted, assaulted tax-collectors, and plundered granaries. Sometimes the peasants were organized and led by *ji-samurai*, small independent landowners of warrior ancestry who possessed efficient weapons and knew well how to use them.

These rebellious agrarian bands drove the sho-gun's officers out of whole provinces or deposed the local daimyo and ruled in their stead. After 1400 they grew continuously stronger. In 1428 a peasant uprising threw into uproar most of the provinces near Kyoto. In 1441 rebellious farmers invaded the capital itself and defied the now powerless shogunate. In several provinces lower-class members of Amidist sects armed themselves and overthrew the feudal lords. Conspiring merchants cornered rice and threatened Kyoto with starvation. Robbers and hoodlums swarmed on the streets in daylight, broke into houses or set them afire. It was a time, in the shocked Japanese phrase, of "the low oppressing the high".

During the period of almost total disorganization, Japan's government was headed by a man who typified the quixotic Ashikaga: Yoshimitsu's grandson, Yoshimasa, who became shogun in 1449. He was a remarkably ineffective ruler; indeed, he did hardly anything in the way of governing except to issue reckless decrees of debt cancellation that only increased the confusion. He was much influenced by women, both by a bevy of favourite mistresses and by his rapacious wife. This shrewd and unscrupulous woman was permitted to pad her private income generously by manipulating the rice market and accepting bribes from nobles and commoners alike. Nor did Yoshimasa stop her from levying illegal taxes; in one instance she amassed large sums by appropriating money levied for alleged repairs of the Imperial Palace. A popular saying of the day claimed that into her grasp poured the "wealth of the realm".

In spite of such failings Yoshimasa is remembered affectionately by many modern Japanese, for he was a sincere patron of the arts, far outdoing any previous shogun. It was in his day that the cultural renaissance, begun in Kyoto's luxurious Muromachi section more than half a century earlier, attained its greatest brilliance. In

Yoshimasa's palaces, amid carefully displayed masterpieces of Chinese painting, porcelain and calligraphy, gathered the leading artists and intellectuals of the time. The shogun did more than merely encourage these creative people; his enthusiasm for Zen principles of aesthetics actively influenced them and helped to establish a quiet, restrained style of art that still prevails in Japan.

Some of Yoshimasa's activities, however, were anything but restrained. Among his extravagances were his festivals, which, according to a contemporary record, almost bankrupted the country. The record's description of one of them makes clear why they were so costly: "A feast of a thousand delicacies was prepared for the flower-viewing excursion. The shogun's attendants were supplied with eating sticks of gold, while the other guests received sticks carved from scented wood and inlaid with precious metals. People ran about madly preparing their costumes. So great was the expense, that they were forced to put all their holdings in pawn and to sell their valuables. Taxes were levied on people in the provinces, and collection of the land and household taxes was pressed. Farmer and landlord suffered dreadfully. Without the means to continue planting and harvesting, they abandoned their fields and turned to begging and lived on whatever their hands and feet could bring them. Most of the hamlets and villages throughout the country reverted to uncultivated fields".

Yoshimasa was also the first great patron of the tea ceremony, that remarkable complex of subtleties that is peculiar to Japan. The ceremony is essentially a quiet meeting of friends with similar aesthetic interests who gather to drink tea while admiring objects of art displayed by their host. It is the ritualized manner in which this meeting is conducted that gives it significance and great beauty. The setting is preferably a special small building, plain but artistically furnished, tucked in the corner of a carefully planned garden. Only a few guests are invited, and the host serves a meal and later the tea itself in a slow, formal way that takes several hours and gives time for leisurely appreciation of the art objects from his collection. This charming ritual, dating from the Muromachi period, survives in modern Japan almost as strongly as ever, although nowadays young girls are also trained to serve tea in the prescribed manner, making the most of fine utensils, costumes and graceful motion.

The tea that provides the focal point of the ceremony is of Chinese origin (the Chinese originally drank it mixed with salt, ginger or even onions), but a popular myth attributes its discovery to that Indian monk, Bodhidharma, who stared at a blank wall in meditation for nine years before becoming a Buddha. Legend says that he was troubled by sleep during his long devotions and to forestall this he cut off his eyelids and threw them on the ground. They took root and grew into tea bushes whose leaves made a drink that banished sleep. Only later was tea admired for its taste and aroma. The early monks were more attracted, like Bodhidharma, by the sleep-preventing caffeine that it contains.

Buddhist monks brought tea to Japan long before Zen became a popular sect, but it was in Zen monasteries that its ceremonial use became important. At first a few monks or disciples who were good friends gathered in a plain, austere room and drank boiled, powdered green tea out of a common bowl before an image of a Buddha. Their words during this communion, if they spoke at all, were low pitched, and their mood, although sociable, was akin to the meditation that dominated early Zen.

This simple ceremony developed during the Muromachi period into an elaborate cult that had great influence on Japanese art, architecture and

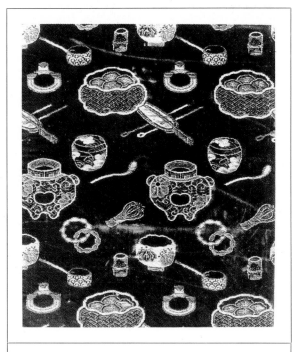

THE FINE ART OF SERVING TEA

The Japanese tea ceremony, as developed by Zen masters in the 15th century, is primarily an aesthetic experience. It follows a ritual as formal and exquisite as a classical ballet. The utensils, many of which are depicted in the piece of brocade above, are often treasured art objects, and the rules for handling them are strict.

Water for brewing the tea is heated in a two-handled iron urn (*middle row of the brocade*) over a charcoal fire. Extra charcoal is kept in wicker baskets (*bottom row*). Using a wooden dipper (*above baskets, to left*), the tea master scoops hot water into a small bowl (*left of dipper*), into which he has spooned a special kind of green tea, taken from a lacquered caddy (*above urn, to right*). He froths the mixture with a whisk (*left of urn*) and decorously passes it to the first guest. Each guest bows to the others, takes exactly three sips and passes the bowl to his neighbour, after cleaning its rim with a tissue. A delicate regard for cleanliness is an important part of the tea ceremony, which according to one master is designed "to cleanse the senses ... so that the mind itself is cleansed from defilements".

social customs. In Yoshimasa's circle its religious element was outweighed by aesthetic appreciation. The Zen monks who advised the shogun encouraged him to make a lavish collection of pictures and ceramics, some of them very old, for his friends to discuss and admire while enjoying their tea. The ritual was usually held in a small, plain room in a building near the so-called Silver Pavilion, which Yoshimasa built on Higashiyama Hill outside Kyoto. This tea-room, which still survives, is considered the prototype of all later Japanese tea-rooms, and its simple but tasteful design is reflected in Japanese houses even today.

Most of Yoshimasa's treasures are still preserved. Through centuries of war and destruction they have been hidden, protected, hurried out of danger. Careful records have been kept of their owners and adventures. Though most of these "Higashiyama pieces" are small and unpretentious, they are now virtually priceless. Probably the most famous is a pottery tea jar. It is only four inches high, and except to true connoisseurs it is not impressive. But the Zen patriarch Dogen brought it with him when he returned from his studies in China in 1227, and for the antiquity-loving Japanese this is enough to make it a national treasure.

The admiration of simple but elegant beauty fostered by the tea ceremony became a strong influence on a number of Japanese arts around Yoshimasa's time. Aesthetic appreciation was then no longer limited to effete aristocrats and monks' circles, as it had largely been in earlier ages. Now warrior barons in the provinces became connoisseurs not only of fine swords but also of paintings and delicate porcelains, and rich merchants spent huge sums to collect rare objects of art.

An important art that came to flower under Yoshimasa's patronage was ink painting, the severely simple renderings in wash and line that rank among the finest accomplishments of the Japanese. The paintings, usually idealized and impressionistic representations of landscapes, figures, birds and flowers, drew their technique and inspiration from similar Chinese art. But in characteristic fashion, Japanese artists modified the Chinese heritage, imbuing their work with a vitality that was all their own.

Among the great masters of this kind of painting was a Zen monk named Sesshu, who in Yoshimasa's day set the standards for all later Japanese ink painters. Sesshu is especially famous for his superb landscape scrolls. Two of these sweeping panoramas of water, mountains and snow-dappled temples still survive, the longer measuring some 55 feet; they epitomize the restraint and subtle simplicity admired and encouraged by Yoshimasa. A few deft, bold strokes of the brush sketch a tree bent by the wind and the jagged rocks beneath it; ships float on a misty lake or sea; against a sky of delicately graded washes the peaks of distant mountains are often scarcely more than a suggestion.

Another kind of art to benefit from Yoshimasa's patronage was the distinctive Japanese drama called No, a uniquely native theatre form that still lives in modern Japan. The No play had developed under previous Ashikaga shogun into a highly refined and stylized entertainment from dancing and singing performances popular in Heian times or earlier. With Yoshimasa's enthusiastic and liberal support it received still further polish. Presented on a simple stage without any special scenery, that play was usually (as it is today) an historical romance combining the music of drum and flute with dancing, beautiful costumes, poetic dialogue and symbolic pantomime. The masks of the principal actors were often masterpieces of sculpture that represented not only human but also supernatural characters. So attracted was

Yoshimasa to this sophisticated form of entertainment that he made No performances outstanding Court occasions; in 1464 a performance attended by the shogun and his high officials lasted for a full week, several plays being given on each alternate day.

It is perhaps symbolic of the character of the artistic but also belligerent Japanese that while the aesthete shogun, Yoshimasa, was communing with artists, poets and playwrights and elaborating the nuances of the tea ceremony, the violence of Japanese politics hit a horrible climax. In 1467 began the Onin War, the prelude to a bloody era of civil strife—*Sengoku Jidai*, the Age of the Country at War—which was to last until the end of the 16th century. The pretext for the Onin War was a dispute over the selection of Yoshimasa's successors. No principles were involved, not even pretended devotion to the emperor or shogun. The war was no more than a greedy struggle for advantage between groups of nobles led by powerful warrior families.

The fighting continued for almost 11 years and was fought mostly in or near Kyoto. Great armies marched to and fro, battling in the streets, burning temples and palaces. Most of the city was destroyed, and much of the population fled. After major battles the streets were choked with corpses, and cartloads of severed heads were collected as trophies. One of Yoshimasa's officials wrote a short poem: "Now the city that you knew has become an empty moor, from which the evening skylark rises while your tears fall".

Yoshimasa's palace and his Silver Pavilion escaped destruction, but when the Onin War finally ended in 1477, the Ashikaga shogun were powerless puppets in the hands of whatever local warlord controlled the capital. The emperors, the puppets of the puppet shogun, were not only powerless but penniless as well. At no other time in Japan's history were they in such dire straits. Their official income had vanished, and they were reduced to selling empty honours whenever they could find a buyer. One emperor is even said to have supported his family by writing out poems in his own elegant calligraphy and selling them to collectors. In 1500, the body of the Emperor Go Tsuchimikado was left unburied for six weeks for want of money for the funeral, and the ceremonial enthronement of his successor had to wait for 20 years because of lack of funds.

With the practical disappearance of the central government went disintegration of the old social order, a process that had long been accelerating as the Ashikaga shogun grew weaker and weaker. In the Age of the Country at War many ancient families were reduced to poverty or exterminated. Those that took their place were often headed by upstart soldiers with little or no aristocratic background. They did not owe allegiance to any great spreading clan like the Taira or Hojo of an earlier day; their families were families in the modern sense, groups of people closely related by blood or marriage, and the ambition of every man was to increase his immediate family's wealth and prestige as much as possible.

This preoccupation forced many social innovations, one of which was a kind of primogeniture. During the stable Hojo régime in the 13th and 14th centuries a landowner had dared to make a will dividing his land among all his children—including the daughters. Even if each received only a little land and therefore had few retainers, the firm power of the Hojo government would protect him in its enjoyment. But under the now-powerless Ashikaga shogunate such evenhandedness was no longer prudent. If there were too many inheritors, they might not be strong enough to defend themselves individually from greedy aggressors. They

might lose their land, and the family as a whole might sink to a lower social level. This was to be avoided at all cost.

So a new custom developed. A father willed the bulk of his property to one of his sons, not necessarily to the first-born but to the most promising, or even to an adopted son if none of his own sons seemed likely to maintain the family prestige. Daughters were left out almost entirely because they were not considered able to keep land in the family. By the start of the Age of the Country at War the subordination of Japanese women, which went to such extremes in later ages, was already well advanced.

Along with these new inheritance customs, a new and more mature kind of feudalism developed. The rules and relationships were no longer imposed from above as they had been in Hojo times. The ghost of a central government in Kyoto had no power to impose anything. Instead, each daimyo in possession of a self-governing territory made his own laws, which usually combined traditional customs with new regulations to fit the times. Most of these family codes were rigidly autocratic, permitting few rights to anyone except the daimyo, but their regulations were seldom obeyed literally, and the picture of life they present does not give an altogether accurate view of Japanese society as it really was.

Actually, the Age of the Country at War was something of an age of freedom for Japan's lower classes. In some provinces the small landholders banded together, swept aside the laws of the daimyo and got full control of the local government; in others the *ji-samurai* (rural landholders of warrior descent) were so numerous, well armed and belligerent that their wishes, not the daimyo's, had to be respected. Artisans, too, were often better off than they had been; in spite of drastic laws intended to keep them at home, many of them fled their native fiefs for the growing towns, where their skills were better paid.

As the new feudal system took shape, growing from below, Japan came to be divided into many compact, independent domains with well-defined though sometimes shifting boundaries. At the head of each was a warrior daimyo, who may have inherited his position, or won it or increased it in war. Since there was no central power to back him, as in Hojo times, his strength and security now depended altogether on the support of the lesser families holding land in his domain. He defended them and watched over them carefully to see that they did not combine against him or fall under the influence of another lord. In some fiefs the daimyo managed to reinforce the power and prestige of his own family by keeping control of every sale or division of property and every marriage, not only of samurai but also of lower ranks. Lesser families did the same; every smallest decision was made by the head of the family, always trying to keep the family's position as high as possible at the cost of its individual members. Thus, while the Age of the Country at War brought some measure of class freedom, it took away individual freedom; within a family little initiative was possible for anyone but the leader.

For most young men such a system would have been unbearably oppressive except for the outlet of war. Most of the great landholders, and many of the lesser ones too, were always on the prowl, hoping to catch some neighbour at a disadvantage and swallow his territory. And the predatory enterpriser, a chieftain with a reputation for successful aggression, never lacked adventurous young supporters. Not all such recruits were of samurai rank; the georgeous mounted knights of ancient tradition had given way to larger units that included many foot-soldiers armed with spears or other comparatively inexpensive weapons. The warrior barons who led these armies no longer exposed themselves recklessly, as the knights had done, in romantic single combat. The best of them learned to marshal their forces and take advantage of terrain. When they noticed a soldier among their low-born followers who showed talent for this kind of fighting, they might raise him to officer status or even to high social rank. This would have been almost unthinkable in earlier ages, but now there was no power in Japan to tell an independent daimyo what he could or could not do.

When there was no war on land to occupy them, the young fighting men of Japan could find an outlet for their energies in piracy, which was now thriving once more. In the second half of the 15th century fleets of hundreds of pirate vessels were crossing the East China Sea and attacking the whole coast of China. The marauders not only pillaged seaside towns but also penetrated far inland to raid the country around Nanking, 150 miles from the sea.

In their suddenness and ferocity these pirate attacks launched by the Japanese resembled those of the Vikings who burst out of Scandinavia in the 10th century. The two races of sea rover were different in many ways, but both used small, fast ships propelled by a combination of sails and oars, and built to make surprise landings on beaches and river banks. Both were better fighters than most of the people whom they encountered, and both acquired fearsome reputations, inspiring such terror that they often met little resistance.

At first the pirate depredations elicited no forceful reaction from the Chinese. The Ming Court merely prohibited Japanese and all other foreign trade, but this irrational action had chiefly the effect of leading coastal Chinese to join the pirates. Soon the ships of the Wako (a name for Japanese pirates derived from a Chinese epithet meaning "dwarf") were extensively manned by Chinese and Koreans.

Later the Ming government reacted strongly, built a navy of large ships that the Wako could not defeat and fortified many places along the coast. The Wako learned to make their raids with more caution and to combine them whenever possible with peaceful though illegal trade with Chinese ports. The more adventurous pirate admirals led their fleets farther south. They raided the Philippines, sometimes digging up old graves in the hope of finding antique Chinese pottery for use in the tea ceremony back in Japan. They reached Thailand, Java and the Malacca straits between Sumatra and Malaysia.

In the early 16th century the Wako began to make permanent settlements. There were strong Japanese colonies in the Philippines, Formosa, Indonesia, Malaysia, Thailand and what is now Vietnam. The settlers did a good deal of peaceful trading, but they kept their warlike spirit and were often embroiled in local political struggles. At one point, the self-governing Japanese colony in Thailand had grown strong enough to enthrone a Thai king.

The activities of the Wako were exceedingly profitable, and wealth flowed back to their outfitters and protectors, the daimyo of southern Japan. Perhaps the most important of these were the great barons of western Honshu, but many feudal lords of Kyushu and Shikoku were also enriched by the peculiar Wako blend of piracy and trade. Around their strongholds grew prosperous cities that competed to attract artists, poets and scholars away from the rest of Japan.

If nothing had happened to interfere with the Wako expansion, Japan might well have gained permanent control of the Philippines, much of Indonesia and perhaps part of the South-East Asian mainland. But, while the Wako were in their heyday, momentous events on the far side of the earth, known to few if any Japanese, were to alter the course of world history. Europe had just emerged from the long impotence of the Dark and Middle Ages and was reaching out to the greater world. Portuguese navigators were probing down the coast of West Africa, and in 1488 Bartholomeu Dias rounded the Cape of Good Hope. Ten years later Vasco da Gama sailed across the Indian Ocean to the merchant city of Calicut in India, and in 1513 Portuguese ships made their first visit to China. Now the Wako no longer had so clean a sweep of East Asian waters. Instead of lightly armed Arab dhows, there sailed the massive Portuguese carracks, carrying cannon that were capable of sinking any ship that sailed the China Sea.

The Wako must have seen the Portuguese or at least heard of them soon after they arrived in the Far East, but there is no record of what they thought about them. The first Europeans known to have set foot in Japan were three Portuguese adventurers who landed from a junk on the island of Tanegashima south of Kyushu in 1542 (or 1543; the date is uncertain). They carried arquebuses, a matchlock musket that was the latest product of Europe's rapidly developing fire-arm industry.

The Lord of Tanegashima welcomed the three strange-looking foreigners and treated them well, and his interest increased enormously when one of the Portuguese demonstrated the deadly effectiveness of his arquebus. As practised and pragmatic warriors, the Japanese realized at once the importance of this novel weapon, which could kill the fiercest samurai long before he could get within sword range. The lord bought the arquebuses for a generous price, and set his armourers to work making copies of them. Something new and unpredictable had entered the Country at War.

SLIDING SCREENS, *of translucent paper pasted against a delicate wooden lattice, are the doors and sometimes even the walls of Japanese houses. Called "shoji", the screens are fitted into wooden slots, which allow them to be slid open and shut. Occasionally, they are ornamented with simple designs, like the chrysanthemum motif shown here. But even without adornment, "shoji" have a restrained, functional beauty belonging to the finest tradition of Japanese design.*

DESIGNS FOR LIVING

Some things never change in Japan. The most common objects of Japanese life—combs, sandals, fans and umbrellas—survive today in virtually the same forms as developed in the early years of Japanese culture. The kimono worn by a modern businessman home from the office is the same type of loose-fitting garment worn by his ancestors. The sliding paper screens (*above*) that wall his house, and the woven straw matting that covers its floors have been used in Japanese homes for centuries.

The quality that makes these everyday objects survive is economy of design. Most are made from common raw materials—wood, paper and straw left over from winnowed rice. But all have been designed with an eye for beauty—an appreciation of simple, natural forms similar to the aesthetics of Zen Buddism, which emphasizes severity and restraint. Some of these articles are used in the Zen-inspired tea ceremony, which places great value on rustic, utilitarian shapes. All are supremely functional. Because of this conscious blend of simple beauty and utility, these ordinary objects have left a permanent imprint on the texture of Japanese life.

CHOPSTICKS *come in pairs and are among the world's simplest and most versatile eating utensils. They have been used for more than a thousand years in Japan, where they are known as "hashi". They usually measure about eight inches long. Larger varieties are used for cooking and serving, and also for stirring the fire in charcoal braziers. Most "hashi", like the ones shown here, are made out of wood, but bone, ivory, gold and silver as well have been fashioned in the same simple and functional form.*

FESTIVE SWEETS, *in the shape of flowers and leaves, have been served ever since Heian times on ceremonial occasions, such as weddings and formal teas. As with many Japanese delicacies, their appearance is just as important as their flavour. Made from little more than sugar and rice flour, these simple sweets, known as "higashi", are sensitively moulded to form maple leaves, chrysanthemums, cherry and plum blossoms—motifs that are often used in Japanese design.*

A WOODEN DIPPER, *called a "hishaku", consists of an unadorned bowl of cedar wood to which a slender wooden handle has been fitted. This stark simplicity of design makes the dipper an ideal utensil for use in the tea ceremony, which among other things celebrates the beauty of rustic objects. In the traditional ceremony, the dipper is placed beside a stone basin on the path to the tea house. (Often it rests on a rack of bamboo like the one shown here.) Guests use the dipper for scooping up water to cleanse their hands and their mouths before entering the room where tea is served.*

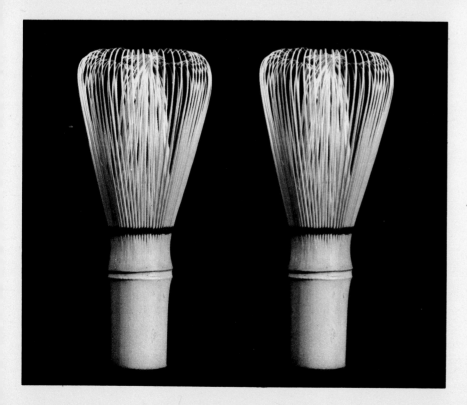

TEA WHISKS, *or "chasen", are made by splitting the ends of short pieces of bamboo into a nest of wire-like loops. They are essential for preparing a variety of powdered green tea commonly used in the tea ceremony. The "chasen" are used to whip a mixture of the powdered tea and hot water into a foaming brew, which sometimes has the consistency of thick pea soup and which has been described by a poet as "the froth of the liquid jade".*

THE FOLDING FAN, *or "sensu", was supposedly invented in the seventh century by a Japanese craftsman who modelled its ingenious construction of pivoted wooden ribs after the folding wings of a bat. "Sensu" quickly became an indispensable part of Japanese life and manners. They were always carried at Court, and emperors frequently handed them out as gifts. Invariably they were ornamented—with a poem, painting, family crest or other design. The dark circle on the fan shown here represents the round of the sun—the traditional emblem of Japan.*

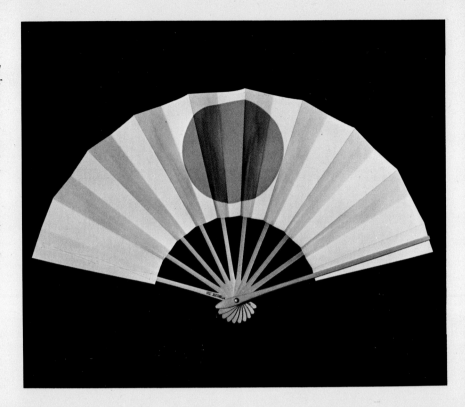

WOODEN CLOGS *came into use as the customary foot-wear for out-of-doors use during the sixth century, when the arrival of Buddhism put an end to the killing of animals for shoe leathers. The clogs, known as "geta", are attached to the foot by a cord that passes between the first and second toes, and they are raised off the ground on blocks. This added elevation not only gave the wearer a statuesque grace; it also had the practical advantage of protecting his kimono from mud.*

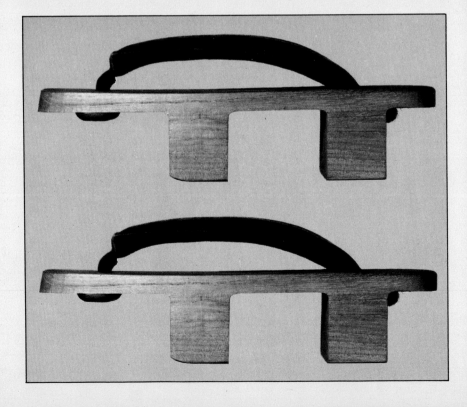

A DECORATIVE KNOT, *made in a special type of coloured string known as "mizuhiki", is the accepted way of tying up gifts in Japan. The exchange of presents has always been an important part of Japanese etiquette; gifts are presented not only at holidays and weddings but also at house-warmings, on the eve of journeys and during ordinary social calls. Over the centuries, special rules have evolved governing the manner in which presents should be wrapped; it is considered vulgar, even insulting, to offer a gift that is improperly tied up.*

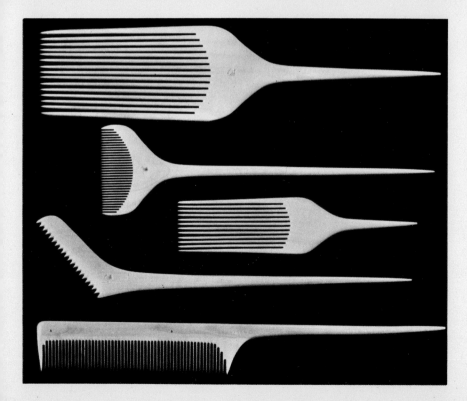

BOXWOOD COMBS, *in a variety of different shapes, are used both to arrange the hair and as ornaments in the elaborate coiffures sometimes worn by Japanese women. Known as "kushi", the combs were very fashionable even before Heian times, when they were regarded as good-luck charms that protected the wearer's virtue. Originally they were adornments only for married women: if a man's wife plucked a comb from her hair and threw it away, it was considered a sign that she wanted a divorce.*

SLIPPERS, *called "zori", are classic examples of economical design. Their woven soles and rope-like bindings are sometimes fashioned entirely from rice straw, the most abundant by-product of Japan's annual rice harvest. Because it is so cheap, rice straw is made into a variety of utilitarian objects. Straw rope is used to bind up farm produce, which is often wrapped in matting of woven straw. Screens and certain articles of clothing—even snowshoes—are made out of straw.*

INTERLOCKING "TATAMI", *floor mats made from woven straw, are among the most distinctive features of Japanese houses. During the Heian period, they were laid out like rugs when needed and folded away when not in use. (The name "tatami" is derived from the Japanese word meaning "to fold".) But later, during the 15th century, "tatami" became virtually permanent flooring consisting of matted rice straw some two inches thick, covered by a smooth surface of woven reeds and bound together at their edges by cloth tape.*

A RUSTIC RAIN-CAPE *made of straw is as practical in use as it is shaggy in appearance. Called "mino" in Japanese, it is still worn by field hands and labourers in the rural areas. Its overlapping straw layers, sewn together at the neck, shed water like the overlapping feathers on a duck; the layers also provide an effective insulation against hot and cold weather. With the "mino", a labourer often wears a conical straw hat that is almost waterproof.*

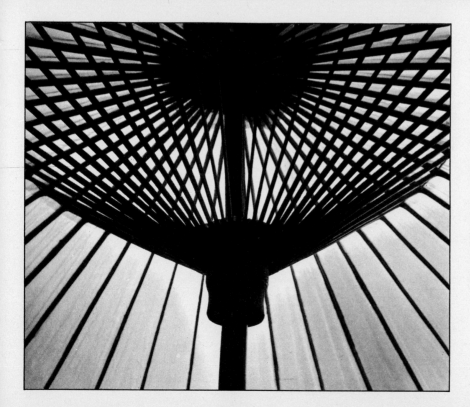

A COLLAPSIBLE PARASOL—*whose intricate framework of bamboo ribs makes a criss-cross design against its water-proof cover of oiled paper—provides efficient protection against both sun and rain. In medieval Japan, parasols, or "kasa", were carried by aristocrats, priests and warriors; later they were affected by courtesans while paying calls on their patrons. The art of fashioning parasols is so highly regarded in modern Japan that today's leading parasol maker has been designated an "intangible cultural property" by the government.*

6

THROUGH
EUROPEAN EYES

With the arrival of Europeans in the mid-16th century, Japanese history and culture come into sharper focus. The foreigners' fresh and wondering eyes saw many fascinating things that Japanese historians of the time took for granted and never bothered to mention. A few of the foreign traders and seamen who visited Japan wrote good accounts of their experiences, but the best observers were the articulate Jesuit missionaries; their reports give a wonderfully vivid view of a country where nearly everything was strange and unexpected.

Far from being contemptuous of what they saw, the Jesuits were highly appreciative, often judging Japanese ways superior to their own. They made great efforts—not always successful—to master the difficult Japanese language, and gave close attention to the intricate formalities that played so important a part in Japanese life. Much of the value of their accounts comes from the fortunate fact that they made their observations when the Japanese were friendly towards Europeans but had not yet been influenced by them. Without the reports of the Jesuits, much less would be known about early Japan.

The first Europeans to reach Japan were the Portuguese. They were delighted to find an Oriental country with a temperate climate whose people they could like and admire. Their experiences with the Indians living near their stronghold at Goa and the natives of Malaysia and the Spice Islands of Indonesia aroused little but contempt. On the other hand, they found that the Chinese treated them like barbarians and showed no desire to fraternize with them. The Japanese seemed agreeably different. They were not only civilized but friendly as well, and although they thought very highly of themselves they were interested in everything the Portugese could show them. European ships and weapons were the leading attractions, but the Japanese were fascinated with Portuguese clothes, food and drink, and they eagerly questioned the new-comers about the Western world. Although the Portuguese had few European wares to offer, the Japanese willingly paid high prices, mostly in silver, for the silks and other luxury goods that the Portuguese brought from China —a trade area closed to the Japanese by the

A RICE-PLANTING CEREMONY, *depicted on a screen, shows rows of women placing seedlings in the paddies to the accompaniment of dancers and a band. This sacred ritual, celebrating Japan's staff of life, was among the colourful customs that impressed early Portuguese visitors to Japan.*

Chinese government because of the depredations of the piratical Wako.

A Portuguese merchant and sea-captain, Jorge Alvares, who visited the port of Kagoshima in southern Kyushu in 1547, was almost ecstatic about what he saw. "It is a beautiful and pleasing country", he reported, "and has an abundance of trees, such as the pine, cedar, plum, cherry, peach, laurel, chestnut, walnut, oak (which yields many acorns).... There is also much fruit not to be found in our country; they grow the vegetables which we have in Portugal, except lettuces, cabbages, drills, corianders and even mint; all the rest they have. They also cultivate roses, carnations and many other scented flowers, as well as both sweet and bitter oranges, citrons (although I did not see any lemons), pomegranates and pears."

Capt. Alvares was an excellent observer. He describes Japanese food, houses, hill-top castles and weapons. He notes the fierce pride of the men and remarks that women go about the streets unchaperoned, which they were not accustomed to doing in Portugal at that time. He is shocked, or pretends to be, by the freedom with which both sexes bathe naked in the sight of passers-by. He was interested in the elaborate etiquette. "The people greatly venerate their king [the local daimyo]", he reports, "and it is reckoned a high honour for the sons of the greatest nobles of the kingdom to serve him.... They like speaking softly, and look down on us for speaking roughly. Etiquette demands that a man receive guests of equal rank by kneeling with his hands on the floor until they are seated. When the king goes abroad, he is attended by his guards. When the people meet him in the streets, they all bow low with their shoes in their hands until he passes. Inferiors do the same for superiors, and if they meet noble and honourable people they take off their shoes and bow very low with their hands between their thighs; when they finish speaking, they cross their arms and depart."

When Capt. Alvares was in Kagoshima harbour, he gave refuge on his ship to a Japanese named Yajiro, who was in trouble on shore, and concealed him and two followers until he sailed. When the ship reached Malacca, he introduced the three to the Spanish Jesuit Francis Xavier, who would later be given the title of Apostle to the Indies. The future saint was delighted with the Japanese and with the captain's descriptions of their country. Here was the ideal land, he thought, for missionary endeavour: a rich, populous, temperate country inhabited by people as civilized as the Chinese but without the Chinese haughtiness.

Xavier took Yajiro and his followers to Goa, where they learned Portuguese and were received into the Roman Catholic faith. In April 1549, a small expedition—Xavier, two other Spanish Jesuits, the three Japanese and two servants—started for Japan. At Malacca they took passage on a Chinese pirate junk, the only craft available. On the 15th August, the Feast Day of Our Lady of the Assumption, the pirates put into Kagoshima, and Xavier went ashore in the land that he dreamed of making the first Christian country in the Orient. He and his companions got a friendly reception from the powerful daimyo of Satsuma, the feudal lord of Kagoshima, who gave them full permission to preach their doctrines and convert whomever they could. They were listened to respectfully by people of all classes, including Buddhist priests, and before they left Kagoshima they had baptized 150 converts.

There is doubt about the depth of these conversions. Xavier by his own account never made much progress in speaking Japanese, and explaining Christian theology through his poorly educated interpreters must have been difficult. Some of the early converts may have been under the impression that they were merely joining a new and interesting Buddhist sect. The two religions have outward similarities—the use of prayer beads, for instance. Even the central idea of a Redeemer is common to Christianity and the Amidist branches of Buddhism. The fact that the Christian Redeemer, Jesus, was crucified was apparently not too repellent to the Japanese. To some it may have been attractive. The most heroic characters in Japanese fiction and real life are those who suffer defeat and death for a noble cause.

Whether Xavier's doctrines were understood or not, he got the same warm welcome in many parts of Japan as he had in Kagoshima, and his first report to his superiors in Goa glowed with enthusiasm. "The people whom we have met so far", he wrote, "are the best who have as yet been discovered, and it seems to me that we shall never find among heathens another race to equal the Japanese. They are a people of very good manners, good in general, and not malicious; they are men of honour to a marvel, and prize honour above all else in the world. They are a poor people in general, but their poverty, whether among the gentry or those who are not so, is not considered a shame. They have one quality which I cannot recall in any people of Christendom; this is that their gentry howsoever poor they may be, and the commoners howsoever rich they be, render as much honour to a poor gentleman as if he were passing rich."

In writing this paragraph, Xavier seems to have been reacting more like a poor and proud Spanish nobleman, which is what he was by birth, than like a disciple of the humble Jesus. He was not at all shocked by the warlike character of the Japanese and he had put his finger on the key of Japanese society: the importance of birth and rank. Succeeding Jesuits followed Xavier's lead. During their 90-year stay in Japan, they con-

centrated on the conversion of the nobles and samurai in expectation that the upper classes' example or command would bring the common people to the Christian faith.

Early in his visit, Xavier became aware of the mysterious emperor who lived in Kyoto and the shogun who was supposed to be his military deputy. No one seemed to obey these shadowy potentates, but Xavier decided that he should visit them nevertheless. He may have thought he could convert all Japan by starting with its rulers, as the Jesuits often tried to do in heretical parts of Europe. In any case he made the long, painful journey on foot to the ancient capital, which he found in turmoil. The shogun was away, and he was told that the powerless emperor was not to be seen. Deciding that he could do nothing in Kyoto, Xavier returned to the friendly communities of western Japan.

Travelling among the daimyo there, Xavier made another observation that would affect Jesuit policy in Japan. He found that every lord who possessed a harbour was eager for Portuguese merchantmen to enter it. These ships were comparatively large and carried effective artillery, and so they offered the only means by which valuable cargoes from China could be ferried across the China seas without great risk of loss to pirates. Even a single cargo of Chinese silk safely landed in a daimyo's harbour brought wealth to him and to his fief.

The value that the Japanese placed on Portuguese shipping gave the Jesuits great leverage in Japan, since the missionaries could exert considerable influence on the Portuguese merchantmen. All during their stay in Japan the Jesuits, whatever their personal nationality, had the powerful backing of the Portuguese crown and its political officials in the Far East. Therefore the Portuguese merchants and seamen were forced to treat them with the greatest deference and, in

A MIGHTY PORTUGUESE SHIP, *shown in a 16th-century Japanese painting, anchors in Nagasaki harbour, while its sailors swing in the rigging and yardarms like monkeys. The Japanese were impressed by the square-rigged ship, since they had no comparable vessels; but they called the Portuguese sailors "namban", or "southern barbarians".*

any case, some of them felt genuine reverence for the missionaries' religious calling.

The Japanese, who lived by elaborate rules of respect for social superiors, noticed the high position of the Jesuits and concluded that they were men of great power among the foreigners and could order Portuguese ships to touch at any harbour that they selected. As soon as the Jesuits became well established, they actually acquired this power, and it was one of the main reasons why they were treated so well by the Japanese.

Xavier left Japan in 1551, never to return.

Later he concluded that the best way to convert the Far East was to start with China, the fountainhead of its civilization, but he did not forget the Japanese, whom he called "the delight of my heart". Other Jesuits replaced Xavier, but the mission grew slowly. In 1560 there were only six missionaries in all Japan, and in 1570 about 20. They soon discovered that Japanese life was not quite as idyllic as Xavier had described it. The expression "Country at War" was no idle phrase. There was no effective central government and peace was not to the taste of the bellicose samurai. Conflicts between feudal lords were apt to break out at any moment, and no place was safe from invasion, pillage and destruction. The Jesuits were held in high respect, and apparently none of them were killed in these bloody tumults, which often amounted to full-scale wars of conquest; but they were often forced to move from one fief to another when a friendly daimyo was displaced by a hostile one.

The Jesuit campaign to cultivate the aristocracy was quite successful. Most of the missionaries were men of high birth whose education and good manners made an excellent impression on Japanese gentlemen. They were not soldiers, but the rigid discipline demanded by the leaders of their order and proudly accepted by the underlings won the admiration of the feudal lords. Throughout their stay in Japan the Jesuits were treated as honoured associates of the ruling class.

Their success in winning actual converts was spotty. Quite a number of aristocrats accepted baptism because they hoped the missionaries would bring trade to their ports and they sometimes commanded their people to become Christians too. If Portuguese ships failed to arrive as expected, these "converts" were apt to backslide; but a good many noblemen did become permanent Christians and communicated their faith to their relatives and associates, and some of the commoners continued to attend the Christian churches even after their feudal lords had recanted. In this way, very gradually, a Christian community grew in Kyushu and to a lesser extent in other parts of Japan, where the Jesuits and their converts were given permission to preach and where they collected small congregations.

Occasionally the missionaries showed an excess of zeal. "God gave such strength to the padres", reported one Jesuit, "that ... they destroyed and burned all the monasteries and temples of the bonzes [Buddhist monks], and converted within a few months all the heathen of those lands, without leaving a single gentile or trace of a bonze, so that our Law and the padres now acquired greater power and prestige than they had done previously." Often such triumphs were short-lived. Some Buddhist sects were corrupt and unpopular, but others had powerful backers and passionate adherents. Sometimes the bonzes rallied and instigated popular revolts to expel the missionaries, or even persuaded neighbouring lords to come with an army and overthrow any daimyo who favoured Christianity.

Such changes of fortune were trying, but the Jesuit leaders seem to have accepted them as unavoidable, for the feudal anarchy that made each Christian success uncertain was, for the time being at least, advantageous to their cause. There was no paramount power to exclude all missionaries from the country. When things went badly for the Jesuits they could always move to another fief and try again, and often they left a good number of converts in the places from which they were expelled.

The Jesuits finally found a secure headquarters by co-operating with Portuguese merchants. As Portuguese trade with Japan increased, it became essential for the silk-laden "Great Ships" to have a safe Japanese base. Most of the harbours along the Kyushu coastline were too shallow or exposed to provide shelter for the clumsy, deep-riding Portuguese carracks, and there was always the possibility that if a captain entered a harbour without being sure of conditions on shore, both his ship and its precious cargo might fall into the hands of some hostile force. Portuguese trade authorities were therefore eager to find a good harbour where their friends were always in firm control, and this was what the missionaries managed to provide.

About 1569, the Jesuit Gaspar Vilela visited a

small fishing village in north-western Kyushu, ruled by a Christian vassal of an important daimyo whom the missionaries had converted and renamed Dom Bartholomew. Father Vilela seems to have appreciated the potential value of the village. Helped no doubt by the daimyo's favour, he converted all the vassal's 1,500 retainers, burned the Buddhist temple and built a Christian church on its site. Soon after these events a Portuguese ship arrived from China and found other parts of Dom Bartholomew's fief blazing with revolt against the Christians. Father Vilela's seaside village remained peaceful, however, and it had a magnificent, deep-water harbour that was easy to defend. After some negotiation, Dom Bartholomew presented the village to the Jesuits as a safe and permanent terminal to Portuguese trade. That village was Nagasaki, which was to grow into an important seaport of modern Japan, and achieve tragic fame in 1945, when it was largely destroyed by the second American atomic bomb.

Nagasaki quickly became a Christianized town with churches, schools and a fort-like Jesuit residence. Its population increased as Portuguese, Chinese and Japanese merchants moved in to enjoy its trade advantages. Christian Japanese driven from hostile fiefs settled in villages near the harbour. The town was governed by a board appointed by the Jesuits, who collected port dues from the shipping and divided them with Dom Bartholomew. The only fault that the missionaries could find with this arrangement, as one of them explained in a letter, was that they could not order the summary execution of law-breakers. Without this power, he said, it was difficult to control a Japanese population.

While settling down in Kyushu the Jesuits wasted no opportunity to study Japan, and the intelligent, lively reports that they sent back to their superiors gave unforgettable pictures of the

"Country at War". Even in the flush of his first enthusiasm Father Xavier noticed the extreme combativeness of the samurai. "The Japanese", he wrote, "have a high opinion of themselves because they think that no other nation can compare with them as regards weapons and valour, and so they look down on all foreigners. They greatly prize and value their arms, and prefer to have good weapons, decorated with gold and silver, more than anything else in the world. They carry a sword and dagger both inside and outside the house and lay them at their pillows when they sleep. Never in my life have I met people who rely so much on their arms. . . . They are very warlike and are always involved in wars, and thus the ablest man becomes the greatest lord."

Among these proud and well-armed people the foreigner did well to mind his manners. Wrote Father Alessandro Valignano, a Jesuit of Italian birth: "I fancy that there are no people in the world more punctilious about their honour than the Japanese, for they will not put up with a single insult or even a word spoken in anger. Thus you speak (and, indeed, must speak) courteously even to the most menial labourers and peasants, because they will not have it otherwise, for either they will drop their work without giving a second thought to what they stand to lose, or else they will do something even worse".

Father Valignano realized, however, that the Japanese had developed an elaborate system of behaviour to keep minor disputes from ending in deadly violence. "In order not to become heated in their dealings with others," he wrote, "they observe a general custom in Japan of not transacting any important or difficult business face to face with another person, but instead they do it all through messages or a third person. This method is so much in vogue that it is used between fathers and their children, masters and their servants, and even between husbands and wives, for they maintain that it is only prudent to conduct through a third person such matters which may give rise to anger, objections and quarrels. As a result they live in such peace and quietness that even the children forbear to . . . hit each other like European lads; instead, they speak politely and never fail to show each other respect. In fact they show such incredible gravity and maturity that they seem more like solemn men than children.''

Father Valignano also recognized that these very courtesies might well cover up a dangerous deceit. "Although two men may be deadly enemies," he wrote, "they will both smile at each other, and neither will fail to perform any of the customary courtesies towards the other. Their conduct in such cases is beyond both belief and understanding; things reach such a pass that when they are most determined to take revenge and kill somebody, they show him much affection and familiarity, laughing and joking with him. Seizing their chance when he is completely off his guard, they draw their heavy swords, which are as sharp as razors, and so attack him that generally he is killed by the first or second blow. Then they replace their swords quietly and calmly as if nothing had happened and do not give the slightest indication of passion or anger either by word of mouth or change of expression. And thus they all give the impression of being mild, patient and well disposed, and it cannot be denied that they are superior to all other peoples in this respect.''

The Jesuits were naturally critical of Buddhism, which they saw as the principal obstacle to their proselytizing. They often denounced the Buddhist monks as greedy and dissolute, as well as being agents of the devil, yet they did not fail to appreciate the touching sentiment of some Buddhist festivals. In 1561, Father Vilela watched with obvious sympathy the Buddhist Day of the Dead.

"They have another festival called *Bon*," he wrote, "held each year in the memory of the souls of their forebears. . . . Everybody sets lighted lamps in the streets, decorated as best he can, and all night long the streets are thronged with people, some out of devotion to the dead, and others out of curiosity to see what is going on. On the evening of this day of All Souls, many people go outside the city to receive the souls of their ancestors and, reaching a place where they imagine that they can meet the souls they have come in quest of, they begin to converse with them. Some offer them rice, others vermicelli, whilst those who are very poor proffer hot water, together with many offerings, saying unto them 'come and welcome! We have not met for a long time; you must be tired, pray be seated and eat a little', and such-like words. They then place what they have brought on the ground, and wait for about an hour, as if to give their unseen guests time to rest and eat. This done, they ask them to come home, and say they will go on ahead to make ready for them. Returning to the house, they arrange a table after the fashion of an altar, whereon they place rice and other foodstuffs. . . . For no matter how poor they may be, everybody offers what he can to the souls of his forebears, and whosoever does not is regarded as beyond the pale.''

If the Jesuits admired, with reservations, certain native religious customs, they expressed delight over Japanese table manners. "They are much amazed", wrote Father João Rodrigues, "at our eating with the hands and wiping them on napkins, which then remain covered with food stains, and this causes them both nausea and disgust.''

Japanese customs were much more civilized. "It is hard to imagine", wrote Father Valignano, "what their food and drink is like, and how it is served, for they observe much cleanliness and solemnity at table and are quite unlike us. Each person has his own table, but there are no tablecloths, napkins, knives, forks or spoons. All they have are two small sticks, called *hashi*, which they manipulate with such cleanliness and skill that they do not ... let even a crumb fall from their plate on to the table. They eat with such modesty and good manners that they observe just as many rules at table as they do in other things".

Far more exotic to the Jesuits than ordinary meals was the elaborate tea ceremony. "It is customary with the noble and wealthy Japanese," wrote Father Luis d'Almeida, "when they have an honoured guest ... to show him their treasures as a sign of esteem. These treasures consist of the utensils they use in drinking a certain powdered herb called *cha*, which is very pleasant to those who are accustomed to drink it .... The caddy in which they place the *cha* leaves, the spoon with which they scoop them, the ladle with which they take the water from the kettle, and the stove—all these utensils form the jewellery of Japan, in the same way as rings, necklaces and ornaments of magnificent rubies and diamonds do with us. And they have experts who appraise these utensils and who act as brokers in selling or buying them. Thus they give parties to drink this herb (of which the best sort costs nine or ten ducats a pound) and to display these utensils, each one as best as his wealth and rank will allow."

Father d'Almeida attended one of these parties at the house of a rich convert whom he calls Sancho. "We emerged into a courtyard ... ", he wrote, "and entered the house where we were to eat. This place was a little larger than the courtyard and appeared to have been built by the hands of angels rather than of mortal men. On one side was a sort of cupboard such as is usual here, and right in front a hearth of black earthenware about a yard in circumference, that shone

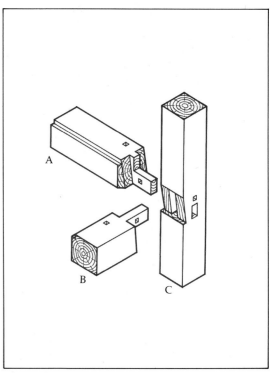

A CAREFULLY FITTED JOINT *between two floor girders (A and B) and a corner column (C) was a sophisticated, 16th-century version of a technique Japanese builders developed in the fifth century. The girders fitted exactly into the corner column and were held in by wooden pegs.*

like the most highly polished mirror.... The ashes on which the glowing charcoal lay looked like finely ground and sifted egg-shells. Everything was exquisitely clean and set out with such order as to be beyond description....

"When we had taken our places, they began to serve the repast. I do not praise the food, for Japan is but poorly provided in this respect; but as regards the service, order, cleanliness and utensils, I can confidently affirm that nowhere in the whole wide world would it be possible to find a meal better served and appointed than in Japan. ... Sancho with his own hands made and served the *cha*, which is the powered leaves I spoke of. Afterwards he showed me, among many others of his treasures, a small iron tripod, little more than a span round, on which they put the lid of the kettle when it is taken off. I took this in my hand. It was so worn with age in parts that it was soldered in two places where it had broken through sheer decay. He told me that this was one of the most valuable of its kind in all Japan,

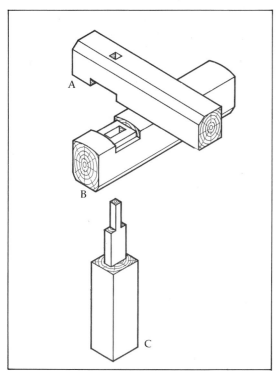

A SUPPORT JOINT, *also made by precise carving, consists of individual pieces that fit snugly. Here an eave's beam (A) is made to fit over a ceiling beam (B). These are locked together by the wall column (C), which comes up through them. Japanese builders still use both techniques.*

and that it had cost him 1,030 ducats, although he personally considered that it was worth much more. All these things were kept in fine damask and silk bags, each in its valuable little box."

One thing Japanese that none of the missionaries admired was Japanese music. Wrote Father Lourenço Mexia, who sounds long-suffering: "Their natural and artificial music is so dissonant and harsh to our ears that it is quite a trial to listen to it for a quarter of an hour; but to please the Japanese we are obliged to listen to it for many hours. They themselves like it so much that they do not think there is anything to equal it in the wide world, and although our music is melodious, it is regarded by them with repugnance. They put on many plays and dramas about various wholesome and joyful things during their festivals, but they are always accompanied by this music."

Much more pleasing to the missionaries was Japanese architecture. Some of their reports of castles and palaces aroused resentment in Rome, where high praise of heathen achievements was not al-ways admired. One such report was written in 1565 by Father d'Almeida after a visit to the castle of the powerful daimyo Matsunaga at Nara.

"This Lord being, as I said, so powerful in wealth and lands, and strictly obeyed," wrote Father d'Almeida, "resolved to build a fortress in this city as is customary with them. For this purpose he occupied a hill and excavated it, the stone being very soft, and made many towers of the same material. In the middle thereof was a large space, about one-third of the circuit of the city of Goa, wherein he sank many wells, since much water was found three fathoms down. He then invited his chiefest and wealthiest noblemen and those of their retainers whom he trusted to build their houses within this circuit.... He began this five years ago, and they all being envious of each other, built the richest and most sumptuous storied houses that can be imagined. ... All these, as likewise the circuit of the castle and its towers, are built with whiter and smoother walls than ever yet I saw in Christendom. For they mix no sand with the lime, but only knead it with a special kind of very white paper which they make for this purpose.... To enter in this town (for so I may call it) and to walk about its streets seems to be like entering Paradise. It is so clean and white that it looks as if all the buildings had been finished that very day.

"I think there can scarcely be a more beautiful sight in the world than this fortress seen from outside, for it is a sheer joy to look on it. I went inside to see its palatial buildings, and to describe them I would need reams of paper, since it does not appear to be the work of human hands.... The walls are all decorated with paintings of ancient stories on a background of gold leaf. The pillars are sheathed with lead for about a span at the top and bottom respectively, and gilded and carved in such a way that everything looks as if it were covered with gold. . . . As for the gardens . . . which I saw in the palace grounds, I cannot imagine anything more delightfully cool and fresh. . . . I am sure that in the whole world it would be impossible to find anything more splendid and attractive than this fortress."

Perhaps Father d'Almeida's superiors in Rome might be excused for suspecting that the missionary was the one who was being converted. But actually the charming palace that he described could serve very well as a symbol of the less-than-perfect state of Japanese society. Only a few years later, Matsunaga's fortress was burned in one of the innumerable wars of the times.

During this period, about 1570, the bloody politics of the "Country at War" was approaching a turning point. Japan's feudal principalities had been virtually independent domains since the end of the Onin War in 1477, and their ruling lords acted like kings and were often called kings by Europeans. They varied a good deal in power and independence, from petty barons whose few retainers lived in poverty to rich rulers of large and fertile provinces. All during the 16th century, the larger domains had tended to grow at the expense of the smaller ones until a few powerful daimyo controlled by possession or alliance the greatest part of the country. Some of them ruled over lands as rich and populous as many European kingdoms, and it is safe to say that most of them were plotting to subdue the others and make themselves the rulers of all Japan. Their immediate motive was undoubtedly greed for power, but at least some of the lords entertained the more honourable ambition of unifying the country.

In spite of its political divisions Japan had the essential attributes of a nation; its people spoke the same language and followed customs that were more or less uniform. They communicated freely; news, fads and innovations spread quickly across the boundaries of the lords' domains. Monks, pilgrims and traders traversed the whole country. The emperor and shogun might be living in powerless obscurity, but they still survived as symbols of unity, and many Japanese dreamed of the time when they would regain their ancient position, and peace would return to the land.

Japan's disunity had been advantageous to the Christian missionaries, who could play the daimyo against each other by offering the prize of Portuguese trade, but it is hard to estimate whether the arrival of the Europeans hastened the unification of the Japanese State. Certainly the Great Ships of the Portuguese made a strong impression, especially with their heavy guns that could sink any Japanese vessel. Here was power in disquieting form, and after Portuguese seamen began to frequent Japanese ports, tales of the threat of the "Southwest Barbarians" must have spread widely. Even before that time, the far-ranging Japanese pirates presumably brought back reports of the odd-looking men from far away who had broken Moslem power in the Indian Ocean, set up trading posts on the coast of China and dominated the Spice Islands of Indonesia. The pirates must have heard that Portugal was one of the smallest European nations and that armed ships of stronger and stranger Westerners were aggressively exploring the oceans of the earth.

Not until late in the 1500's did Japanese in authority show much concern about the menace of the West. Perhaps such fear was more widerspread than the records show. But by the end of the 16th century, open hostility was directed towards both the Christian missionaries and the threatening Western nations from which they came. Once again Japan was to shut itself in. And while doing so, once again it was to become a unified country, ruled by a succession of military dictators.

A POETIC SLICE OF LIFE

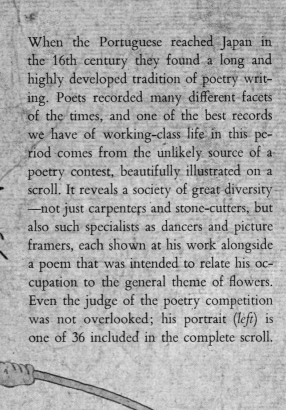

禄
う
ふ
見

ゆ
に
と
も
て
う
か
い
は
ら
せ

万
象

When the Portuguese reached Japan in the 16th century they found a long and highly developed tradition of poetry writing. Poets recorded many different facets of the times, and one of the best records we have of working-class life in this period comes from the unlikely source of a poetry contest, beautifully illustrated on a scroll. It reveals a society of great diversity —not just carpenters and stone-cutters, but also such specialists as dancers and picture framers, each shown at his work alongside a poem that was intended to relate his occupation to the general theme of flowers. Even the judge of the poetry competition was not overlooked; his portrait (*left*) is one of 36 included in the complete scroll.

PHOTOGRAPHED BY T. TANUMA

With cherry blossoms
Out on the first day of spring,
People are restless.
They clamour for spring costumes
To wear viewing spring flowers.

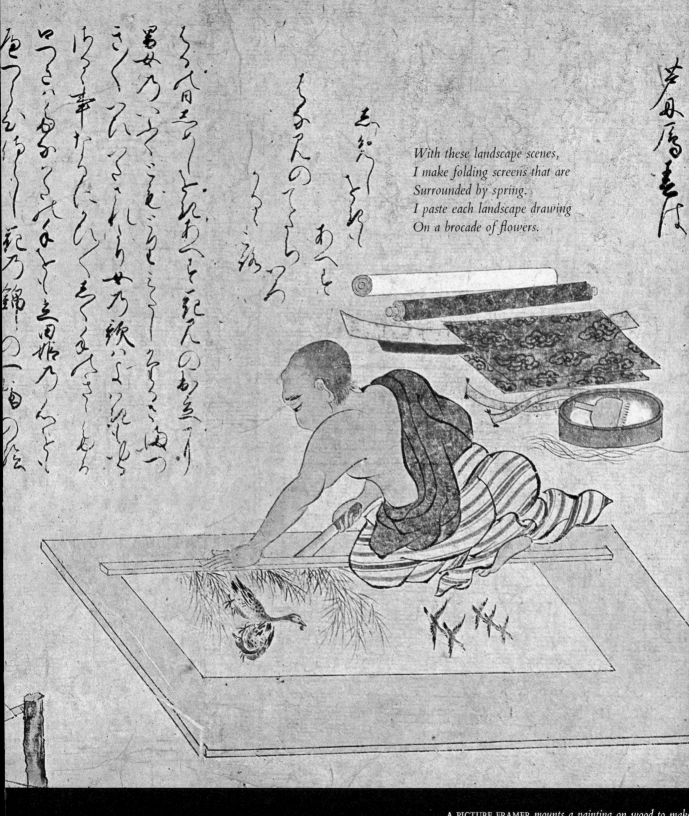

With these landscape scenes,
I make folding screens that are
Surrounded by spring.
I paste each landscape drawing
On a brocade of flowers.

A PICTURE FRAMER *mounts a painting on wood to make*
a folding screen, before matting the picture with a
piece of brocade. These screens were used as dec-
orations and room dividers in wealthy people's houses.

十六番 厄

春くみみぐ
をちらね
る

克狸あろほ
らんじほう
ちろろつる
れて六さ六株
をにとるは
るくなんやう
たのけいくる
めくいい
白騰
うくほうやう

ほうや祁るうら祇
たてぼしきをすて
其をほろきに
見ほうしし

Soon the temple tree's
Branches will be stripped away;
Its bark will be slashed.
Enjoy the tree's aroma,
Its scent of temple incense.

A TREE PEDDLER *walks along selling broad-leafed ev-*
ergreen branches from the sacred "shikimi" tree. The
branches were stripped from the tree and used as offer-
ings at both Buddhist temples and Shinto shrines.

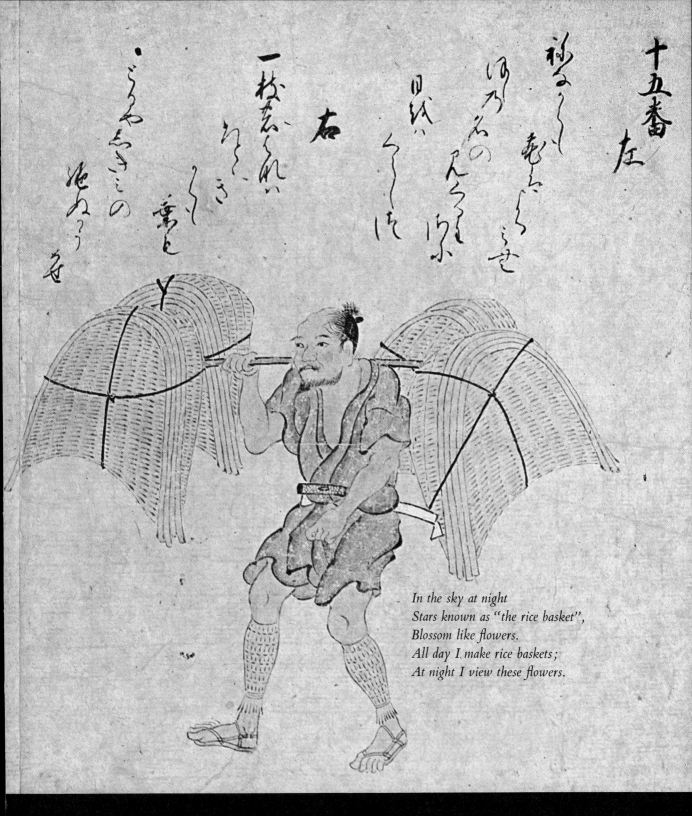

十五番　左

右

In the sky at night
Stars known as "the rice basket",
Blossom like flowers.
All day I make rice baskets;
At night I view these flowers.

A BASKET PEDDLER *sells an item used in every Japanese
house: a rice basket for winnowing, or separating
the grain from its chaff. Rice was not only the staple*

古
あると思ふ
そらる

かこうさりならふ人小れ
みくむなつやや飲谷
離戸へき華するうへ石に
さりつをくらさをこ属る
かよ海こた
地香と
さらふらに
雲冷り
右勝と
とんれ地

When the spring arrives
And I sit outside, working,
I am never bored.
With a chisel in my hand
I can raise flowers from stones.

A STONE-CUTTER *chisels chips as delicate as flower pet-*
als from a block of stone. This piece was probably
intended for use as a stepping-stone or a decorative ob-
ject, such as a lantern, for a formal Japanese garden.

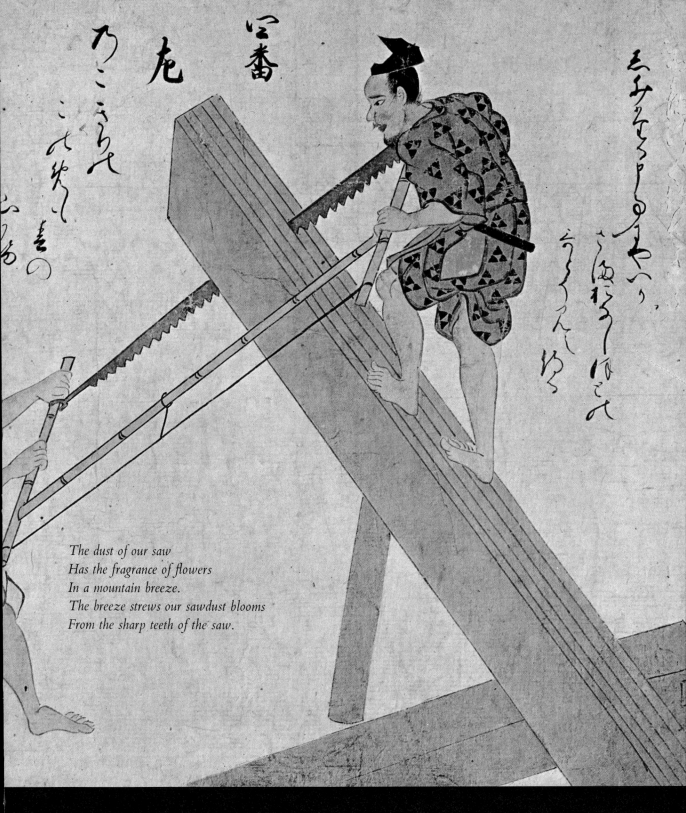

みよや／さらに／なやゝり／うみやゝて／ほさて／うてっえ／ゆら

空番
庵
わこゝられ
これ笑て青の
山青

The dust of our saw
Has the fragrance of flowers
In a mountain breeze.
The breeze strews our sawdust blooms
From the sharp teeth of the saw.

TWO SAWYERS *rip planks from a piece of wood, guiding*

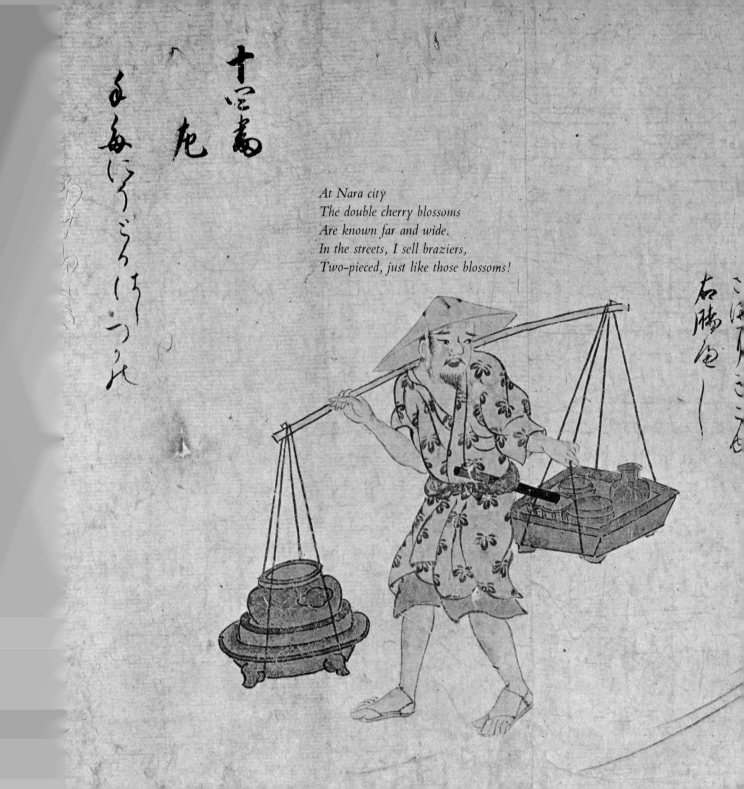

At Nara city
The double cherry blossoms
Are known far and wide.
In the streets, I sell braziers,
Two-pieced, just like those blossoms!

I start work in spring
Making willow-wood buckets
With no time for rest.
Now and then I steal a glance
At the orange-tree blossoms.

志ゝ文珠寺筆跡
さるハ山王の村火者
龍亜源乃勝坊之
ろゝきに花の春滝わ
夜いつてしあを子つて
そにつて人々らし唐
へろこ楊在去去一代
ぬりひにはぬ字ゝ大枝と
拾在虎ゝ我わられ而
孔乃後とろく唐こゝゝれ
んれてし傷水やの自大騰ゝ

This monkey, once free,
Would shake the branches to make
The blossoms scatter.
For their sake I tie him up
To keep him out of the trees.

A MONKEY TRAINER, *carrying a stick to keep his pet in line, was a popular figure who appeared at festivals, where his monkey performed tricks. He was also called upon to entertain tired workmen on the job.*

二番
さ
さつれて
春乃
末つ末に
暮を〻
もくれ〻に
飛も〻花
や兎
右
やもせ〻

将小つ宋小ら〻

The lion dances
Under the spring tree's shadow
To the drum's cadence.
Flowers will blossom faster
To the cadence of a dance.

A DRUMMER *accompanies dancers dressed as a lion.*
These men were seen at festivals, particularly during
New Year. They marched in parades and also went
from house to house chasing away harmful spirits.

7

THE NATION UNITED

The chaos of the Age of the Country at War was finally brought to an end by two remarkable men, Nobunaga and Hideyoshi, whose vigour and ambition made Japan a unified nation. Neither was a prominent daimyo nor even a member of a leading family. Nobunaga was born a very minor feudal lord, and Hideyoshi was that great rarity in Japanese high politics—a commoner below samurai rank. But both were masters of politics as well as warfare, and they and their successor, Tokugawa Ieyasu, determined the course of Japan for the next three centuries.

In spite of the fact that Nobunaga and Hideyoshi did not come from the top ranks of society, the new period saw no diminution of aristocratic control. The commoner Hideyoshi, in particular, made no concessions to his own humble birth, but went to great lengths to keep the lower classes in their place. In spirit, however, Japan did change from the ways of the old aristocracy. There was during this period a new flamboyance and an outburst of unrestrained art and architecture that was far from the delicate understatement of earlier times.

The first of the great unifiers was a fierce, heartless, single-minded autocrat named Oda Nobunaga, whose family were retainers of aristocratic landholders in the province of Owari near the present city of Nagoya. Gradually the Oda family had increased their estates and influence until Nobunaga's father was important enough to buy an honorific rank from an impoverished emperor. In 1551, when Nobunaga succeeded his father as head of the family, he was not yet 20 years old, and some of his relatives were not willing to accept his leadership. Nobunaga reacted to this challenge with the vigour that was to prove characteristic of him. He raised a rustic army of about 1,000 and took the field against the dissidents. It was a local war, typical of many others fought at the time. In the course of it Nobunaga killed his younger brother, stormed one of the family fortresses and subdued the hostile relatives. That was only a first step. By 1559 he had driven the aristocratic constable out of Owari and made himself master of the province.

In spite of this early success Nobunaga was

still a petty lord, governing a small land that stood squarely in the way of a powerful and ambitious daimyo, Imagawa, who was bent on the conquest of Kyoto. In 1560 Imagawa led an army of 25,000 men towards the capital, where he hoped to take control of the enfeebled shogunate. He did not anticipate much trouble from Nobunaga, and his first encounters in Owari were encouraging. His advance guard captured a fort and sent back seven severed heads as souvenirs; the same day another fort fell. Nobunaga at this time had hardly more than 3,000 men; but in spite of the bad news he refused to go on the defensive, much less try to make a deal. When he learned that Imagawa's main force was resting strung out in a narrow defile, he decided to risk everything on a bold attack, counting on his boyhood knowledge of the country to make up for his weakness. On the 22nd June 1560, he led his small force through a mountain trail that flanked the defile and fell on Imagawa's army, which was taken wholly by surprise and further confused by a blinding rainstorm. The soldiers stampeded up and down the ravine, and one of Nobunaga's followers cut off Imagawa's head.

This battle involved comparatively few men, but it is famous as a turning point of Japanese history. Nobunaga's audacity and triumphant generalship was much appreciated by other commanders. He suddenly became a national figure, and many chieftains came over to his side. The most important of these new allies was a former opponent, the Imagawa officer who had spearheaded the invasion of Owari and collected those souvenir heads. Under the name of Tokugawa Ieyasu, he rose to be a leading general and eventually became the ruler of all Japan.

At this time Nobunaga was still a minor daimyo, at least in terms of territory under his control, but he had some important advantages.

His home province, Owari, abounded in spirited yeomen who loved to fight and owned weapons to fight with. These would make good recruits for the new-style army he planned to create.

Japanese battles in the past had been chiefly multiple fencing matches between skilled samurai swordsmen. But times—and tactics—were changing. Large bodies of common soldiers, armed with long spears and trained to fight in close order, had already proved that they could defeat the noble warriors. So the more progressive samurai gradually gave up knightly single combat and acted as officers leading spear-armed privates.

This change by itself would have been momentous; in Japan the sword of the samurai had been for centuries a quasi-religious symbol and a terror to anyone who tried to oppose a man trained to use it. But a second change, the adoption of fire-arms, was even more drastic. The match-lock muskets that the Lord of Tanegashima bought from Portuguese adventurers in 1542 had multiplied with amazing speed. These simple guns had faults, but they were effective nevertheless, and the Japanese soon found that they were not difficult to manufacture. One Portuguese traveller reported that the armourers of the Lord of Tanegashima turned out 600 of the new weapons in six months after first seeing them.

Fire-arms roused great interest in Japanese military circles. Many soldiers despised them and called them the weapons of cowards, but enterprising commanders took to them remarkably fast, considering the well-known conservatism of the military mind. Gun shops quickly sprang up all over the country and were soon making improved models: guns that threw heavier bullets able to kill a man in armour at a considerable distance.

Besides their virtue of long-range deadliness the new weapons had the advantage of being much cheaper than good swords. They were also easier to use. Long training was unnecessary; and sturdy young peasants could be taught to load and fire a musket in a few weeks. This quality made them doubly attractive to upstart military leaders who lacked large companies of skilled samurai. Nobunaga was one of these, and he quickly realized that muskets were just the weapon for his rapidly growing armies of high-spirited but untrained countrymen. He began to use them early in his career, and at least some of his victories were due to musketry tactics that he developed.

After his great victory over the ambitious Imagawa in 1560, Nobunaga strengthened his position by dealing with neighbouring lords who might attack his rear when he himself marched on Kyoto, as he planned to do. Some of them he placated by the time-honoured method of giving them daughters or younger sisters in marriage. Others he destroyed by direct attack or undermined by promising rewards to their followers.

By 1567 he had achieved a position of such strength that important allies sought his favour. The emperor sent him a secret message praising his victories and begging for help in regaining lost estates; in the same year a claimant to the shogunate, Ashikaga Yoshiaki, asked for Nobunaga's support. On the strength of these two requests, Nobunaga considered himself officially authorized to take control of Japan. He ordered to be engraved on his seal the grandiloquent motto: "Rule the Empire by Force". Alarmed daimyo formed leagues against him, but he brushed them aside in a series of bloody battles. In 1568 he marched into Kyoto with Yoshiaki, whom he installed as shogun.

At first the sophisticated capital treated Nobunaga as an uncouth upstart, but unlike other provincial barons who had occupied the city, Nobunaga held his troops under firm discipline. They did not rape or pillage, and he issued a strict order that guaranteed protection to all civilians. This was something new and welcome in a city that had been trampled by countless unruly armies. Soon even the Court nobles were thinking better of Nobunaga and asking him, as the emperor had done, to help them to get back their estates.

Although in control of the capital and enjoying the important legitimacy that came from control over both emperor and shogun, Nobunaga was not secure. He dominated central Japan, the dozen or more rich provinces around Kyoto, but most of the rest of the country refused to obey him. Even close to Kyoto were strong, hostile communities of warlike Buddhist sects. Some of the monks were mercenaries whom anyone could engage. Others were devoted to their religion and fought to the death to protect its shrines. Nobunaga, who seems to have had no religious sympathies, hated them all, and this is one reason why he proved so friendly to Christian missionaries.

In 1569 the Jesuit missionary Luis Frois was introduced to Nobunaga. To Father Frois's surprise, the cruel master of Kyoto, whom everyone feared, received him with cordial friendliness. His report of the interview gives a living picture of a great but ruthless man, who was seldom as pleasant to his own countrymen as to this alien priest.

"He would be about 37 years old," wrote Father Frois, "a tall man, lean, scantily bearded, with a clear voice, greatly addicted to military exercises, hardy, disposed to temper justice with mercy, proud, a great stickler for honour, very secretive in his plans, most expert in the wiles of warfare, little or nothing disposed to accept reproof or advice from his subordinates, but greatly feared and respected by everyone. He does not drink wine, he is rough-mannered, contemptuous of all the other kings and nobles of Japan whom he addresses brusquely over his shoulder as if they were inferiors.... He is a nominal adherent of the Hokke [Lotus] sect, but he openly proclaims that there are no such things as a Creator of the Universe nor immortality of the soul, nor any life after death. He is extremely refined and clean in his dress ... not even a prince dare appear before him with a sword..."

The Jesuits' first interview with this uncompromising character was conducted on the site of a castle being built for the puppet shogun. Nobunaga was striding around with a tiger-skin robe thrown over rough clothes supervising the construction, which employed some 25,000 men. The pious Father Frois was delighted to note that much of the stone for the castle was coming from shrines of the infidel Buddhists. "As there was no stone available for the work," he wrote, "he ordered many stone idols to be pulled down, and the men tied ropes around the necks of these and dragged them to the site. All this struck terror and amazement in the hearts of Kyoto citizens, for they deeply venerated their idols."

Father Frois had had the good fortune to meet Nobunaga soon after the Japanese ruler had declared full war on the Buddhist sects. He regarded them as the principal threat to his supremacy, and therefore the missionaries of the foreign, anti-Buddhist religion may have seemed welcome allies, or at least sympathizers. He favoured Father Frois with many long interviews, during which he questioned the priest about Portugal and Europe and discussed Christianity. Finally he issued a decree that in effect gave the Jesuits authority to live in Kyoto and preach Christianity freely. The Buddhists were furious, but they were in no position to do anything about it. Nobunaga was determined to destroy their power.

In 1571 Father Frois reported with obvious satisfaction the destruction of the ancient religious centre on Mt. Hiei, north of Kyoto. This was one of the holiest places in Japan, sacred to both Buddhist and Shinto gods, but its rich and powerful prelates had offended Nobunaga by supporting his enemies. He assembled an army of 30,000 men and surrounded the mountain. The monks tried to buy him off with 500 bars of gold. When he refused they retreated to the great temple of the Shinto god Sanno on the top of the mountain and took with them most of the inhabitants of their tributary villages.

Father Frois describes what happened next: "Knowing that he had them all on the top of the mountain, Nobunaga immediately gave orders to set fire to Sakamoto and to put to the sword all those found within the town.... And in order to show the bonzes [monks] the little regard he paid to the chimeras (which they had described to him) of the punishments of Sanno, the second thing he did was to burn all the temples of this idol ... he also destroyed by fire the seven universities so that nothing at all was left of them. Then ... he gave the order to advance to the top. The bonzes were unable to resist such a furious assault and were all put to the sword, together with the men, women and children of Sakamoto".

The bloody massacre on Mt. Hiei was only a sample of cruelties to come. Nobunaga attacked the Buddhists wherever he could find them. On the west coast of Honshu he built a wall around one stubborn stronghold, set fire to the encircled area and burned up 20,000 people who had taken shelter in it. When provincial lords came to the help of the Buddhists, his new-style army defeated them easily.

One of these actions against the daimyo, the Battle of Nagashino in 1575, is a landmark in the history of Japanese warfare. Nobunaga took his stand with a paltry force of 3,000 musketeers and awaited the attack of traditional samurai cavalry. The gorgeously armoured horsemen came in waves, swinging their terrible swords, and each wave was mowed down by a disciplined volley.

Not all the musketeers fired at a time: after one group had discharged its weapons, it stepped back to reload while another group made ready to fire. When the musketeers had slaughtered four waves of horsemen, the battle was over.

Other commanders learned this lesson well. Cavalry troops became ceremonial fixtures, rarely used in action, and the musket became the preferred weapon. Those monasteries that Nobunaga had not yet destroyed set up gun shops, and the free city of Sakai became a busy arsenal ready to sell to all buyers. It can be argued that in 1575 Nobunaga's armies were more advanced in the rational use of small arms than any army in Europe.

After the Battle of Nagashino, Nobunaga's most troublesome opponent in central Japan was the great Honganji monastery at Osaka, the holy centre of the rich and powerful Amidist sect. It was strongly fortified and supported by devoted sectarians in many parts of the country. Nobunaga besieged it, and to cut it off from the sea he used ships armed with small cannon and protected with iron armour. These "iron-clads" preceded by nearly 300 years the *Monitor* and *Merrimac* of the American Civil War.

The Honganji monks finally surrendered after being urged to do so by the emperor, whose intervention saved face for them and trouble for Nobunaga. But the Amidist power was broken, and Nobunaga was master of Osaka.

Though Nobunaga fought almost continuously, he also showed considerable skill in non-military statecraft. He well understood the value of working inside the traditional forms. One of his first moves on entering Kyoto was to rebuild the dilapidated Imperial Palace and provide the emperor with sufficient income to maintain a proper magnificence. For a while he also supported his puppet shogun, Yoshiaki, but drove him into exile when he showed a tendency to act on his own. That

MILITANT MONK *with his lethal swords at hand was one of the defenders of the tem-* *at Honganji, which resisted Nobunaga's attempts to conquer it for 11 years.* *ese monks, who spent much of their time making their own weapons and practis-* *archery and musketry, believed that death in battle was a means of salvation.*

was the end of the Ashikaga shogunate, and Nobunaga would have curbed the emperor also, if it had been necessary. He told Father Frois: "Do not worry about either the emperor or the shogun. I am in complete control of everything".

More than most of the military lords, Nobunaga appreciated the importance of trade and finance. He did not attempt to conquer the commercial city of Sakai, but instead made friends and supporters of its richest merchants, so that the city became his dependable source of fire-arms, ammunition and other war materials. He also understood the role of show and pageantry. He raised the morale of his low-born soldiers by dressing them in handsome uniforms and drilling them to march in formation. Both ideas may have been European, and a grand review of his troops that he held in 1581 may have been similarly inspired. His generals were told to appear in their most brilliant costumes to lead a troop of 20,000 horsemen at full gallop past the emperor's reviewing stand.

This splendid ceremony marked the peak of Nobunaga's career. A year later he was dead. In 1582 his generals were still fighting daimyo, who were still holding out, but they were making good progress, and Nobunaga was planning to take part in the final campaigning. His end came suddenly. While lodging in Kyoto, he was surrounded at dawn by the soldiers of Akechi Mutsuhide, a supposedly loyal general. Father Frois tells what happened: "When Akechi's men reached the palace gates they entered at once, as nobody was there to resist them because there had been no suspicion of treachery. Nobunaga had just washed his hands and face and was drying himself with a towel when they found him and forthwith shot him in the side with an arrow. Pulling the arrow out, he came out, carrying a *naginata*, a weapon with a long blade made after the fashion of a scythe. He fought for some time, but after receiving a shot in the

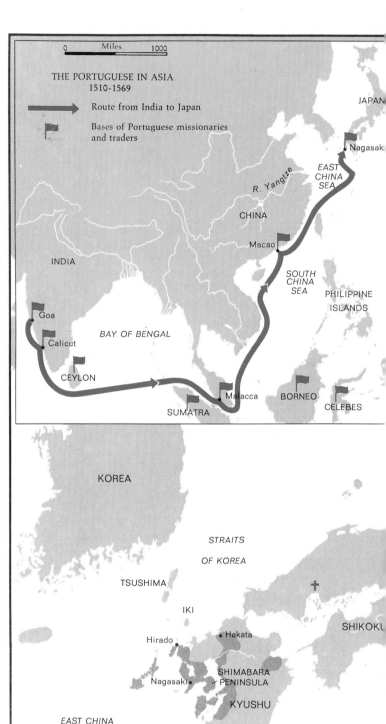

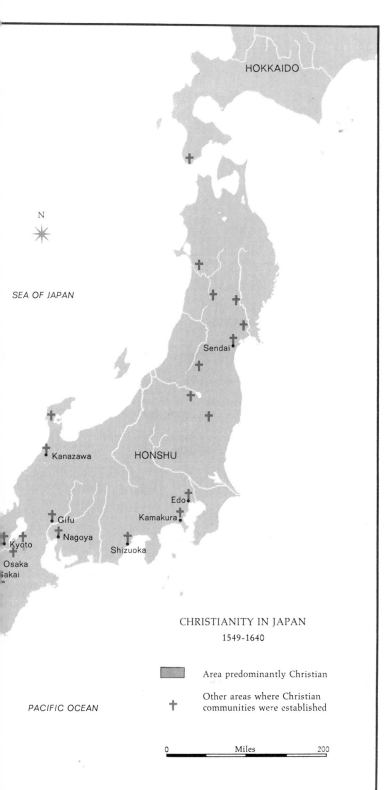

CHRISTIANITY IN JAPAN
1549-1640

▓ Area predominantly Christian

✝ Other areas where Christian communities were established

0   Miles   200

FOR TRADE AND THE CHURCH *Portuguese explorers established bases in India and South-East Asia; in 1549 they reached Japan. From their centre in Nagasaki the missionaries spread Christianity throughout the land. By 1614 they claimed 300,000 converts, but in the following years the government severely persecuted Christians and by 1640 all Portuguese had been ousted.*

arm he retreated into his chamber and shut the door. Some say that he cut his belly, while others believe that he set fire to the palace and perished in the flames. What we do know ... is that of this man, who made everyone tremble not only at the sound of his voice but even at the mention of his name, there did not remain even a small hair which was not reduced to dust and ashes".

Nobunaga was an excessively cruel tyrant, but his loss was a serious blow to the Jesuits, who had welcomed his protection. At his death they claimed only about 150,000 converts. Many of these had been forced to convert by their feudal lords, and even if all had been genuine Christians, they would have formed a negligible part of the Japanese population, which then numbered some 20 million. Still, the missionaries' project was not going badly, and the future looked bright. Their stronghold in Nagasaki was growing and prosperous; their enterprises in the Portuguese trade with China were yielding large revenues, and they had numerous supporters in the high aristocracy. Their schools were beginning to turn out Japanese priests and some of these had become members of the Jesuit order. Now, however, their powerful patron, Nobunaga, was gone, and his successor could hardly be as favourable as he had been.

The successor was Hideyoshi, whom many Japanese consider the greatest man their nation has produced. He was Nobunaga's leading general, and he had been conducting a long campaign against recalcitrant daimyo in western Honshu. On hearing of his leader's murder, he hurried back to Kyoto and in seven days killed Nobunaga's assassin and outmanœuvred Nobunaga's two sons. A rival general, who was Tokugawa Ieyasu, also a Nobunaga favourite, withdrew to the eastern provinces, leaving Hideyoshi master of central

Japan. Many conservative Japanese must have been shocked by his success, for he was the son of a common soldier of peasant origin. In all Japanese history no man of such low birth had ever risen as high.

Hideyoshi had plenty of fighting still to do, but he knew the value of timely compromise. He conciliated Ieyasu by giving him charge of the eastern provinces, and made bloodless peace with several daimyo still holding out.

Even before he was master of all Japan, Hideyoshi began to consolidate his power by means of far-reaching political moves. Through a variety of repressive laws, he set out to freeze the country in a rigid feudal pattern and especially to prevent the rise of other ambitious commoners like himself. The chief targets of his laws were the armed peasants and small landowners who had never been as free or as prosperous as in the late 1500's. During the civil wars many of them had banded together to defy feudal overlords and chase tax collectors out of their villages. Those who had good weapons were too dangerous to molest without the support of a large army.

Hideyoshi himself had been born a member of this large and obstreperous class, but he showed no sympathy for them; he saw clearly that they were a threat to the military aristocracy to which he now belonged, and he moved firmly to hold them down. His first step was a survey assessing all lands in terms of productivity. The job took many years and was bitterly resisted by the country people, who realized only too well that it was intended only to determine the maximum revenue that could be squeezed out of them. Along with the survey went Hideyoshi's "sword hunt": a round-up of all commoners' weapons, including all fire-arms. The villagers were told that the metal in their surrendered weapons would be used to construct a gigantic statue of Buddha and so promote their welfare in the life to come.

To make doubly sure of social stability, Hideyoshi encouraged all daimyo to publish rigid codes designed to keep every member of the population in his proper place. Peasants must not leave their land on pain of severe punishment. Village artisans must not move to a city, and if one of them "absconded", his relatives would be punished, often by death.

In practice the new social system could not have been as repellent as it looks on paper. While it hit the peasant farmers hard it permitted a good deal of freedom in towns and cities. The truth was that, in spite of the ceaseless fighting under Nobunaga, Japan was progressive and prosperous, and it became even more so when Hideyoshi began to enforce order. Production of food increased; towns and villages that had been burned were quickly rebuilt. The new taxation system, rigorously applied, funnelled a swelling stream of revenue into the treasury, and Hideyoshi found himself in control of unexpected wealth, which he invested in castles and palaces more gorgeous than any that Japan had ever seen before.

Hideyoshi was expansive and convivial, altogether a more agreeable person than Nobunaga. He was not notably cruel; he liked wine and entertainment and collected pretty young concubines in large numbers. He was hardly an educated man, but he sought to be considered a patron of the arts and gathered around him the country's leading painters, poets and actors.

During his rule the Momoyama period of art (named after one of his palaces) came to flower. Is has been called Japanese rococco; its character was probably determined by the confident spirit of the age and by the new wealth that peace, national unity and foreign trade had made possible, but Hideyoshi's flamboyant personality may have had something to do with it, too. Gone was the severe and subtle simplicity of Ashikaga times. Momoyama paintings glowed with bright colours, often against backgrounds of gold leaf. Gone were the restraint and discipline preached by Zen Buddhism. Momoyama painting gloried in a riot of detail that sometimes overwhelmed by sheer exuberance the general effect of the composition.

Momoyama buildings, too, were anything but austere. Castles were lined with intricate wood carvings, many of which were covered with gold leaf. Even more ostentatious were the furnishings of Hideyoshi's favourite residence, Osaka Castle. According to one visitor, the common utensils and fittings—kettles, bowls, locks and hinges—were of gold. Hideyoshi's bedroom was 54 feet square. The bed was eight feet long, with scarlet bedding and a headboard encrusted with gold.

Hideyoshi was not at all interested in religion as such, but he was just as much opposed to the Buddhists as Nobunaga had been, and so it was with considerable hope that the Jesuits began to cultivate him. They noted with pleasure that many converted daimyo were his intimates, and when the Court physician, who was considered one of the leading scholars of Japan, was converted too, they began to feel that Nobunaga's death had not been too great a loss for the Christian cause. Hideyoshi pleased them further by visiting their church in Kyoto and chatting with the presiding priest. The only thing he really disliked about Christianity, he explained, was its opposition to a man having many women. "If this could be changed," he said, "I will become a convert."

The Jesuits could not promise to alter this detail of their faith, but they felt that the new dictator was nevertheless a friend, and this impression was reinforced in 1586 when Father Gaspar Coelho, the vice-provincial of their order, visited Osaka Castle. Hideyoshi himself showed the Christian party around his gorgeous palace, preceded,

as the alert Father Frois reported, "by a richly dressed young girl who carried his sword on her shoulder, and with whom he chatted from time to time". After the tour of the castle, Hideyoshi renewed the special rights and privileges that Nobunaga had granted to the Jesuits. He also told them about his plan to invade and conquer China, and he made the padres a surprising offer. If they secured for this adventure the use of two large Portuguese ships, he would promise to build churches all over China and order all Chinese to become Christians.

Father Coelho then made what was later considered a bad mistake. He promised not only the Portuguese ships but also other help from Portuguese India, and he offered to bolster Hideyoshi's influence over the Christian daimyo of Kyushu. Hideyoshi seemed pleased, but the more experienced Jesuits were uneasy. One of them, Father Alessandro Valignano, later conjectured that Hideyoshi was thinking: "This father-provincial is very rich and influential. One day he will make war against me as did the abbot of the Honganji against Nobunaga".

In spite of these forebodings, the Jesuits noted that Hideyoshi seemed to remain as friendly as ever. Then, only a few months after the Christian party's visit to Osaka, he suddenly changed his attitude and ordered all the missionaries—more than 100 of them now—to leave Japan. Father Coelho tried pleading, but this seemed only to infuriate Hideyoshi. Then the vice-provincial made the mistake of asking for military help from the Portuguese in Macao and Goa and the Spaniards in the Philippines, and by trying to organize a league of Christian daimyo to resist the expulsion order. Much of this was almost certainly reported to Hideyoshi, who insisted that the missionaries take the first Portuguese ship out of the country.

This decree of expulsion was never enforced.

Only a few Jesuits actually left Japan; the rest went into hiding for a while and then emerged to carry on their proselytizing as inconspicuously as possible. They observed that their restraint seemed to statisfy Hideyoshi, but they debated long and earnestly the reasons behind the expulsion decree. Some Jesuits thought it was merely an impulsive act. Others feared it indicated suspicion that the Christians were a threat to Japan's newly gained unity, or even to its independence.

This latter thesis certainly seems logical. By 1587 the Japanese knew a good deal about the Western world. Some of them had visited Europe, and what they saw there could not have been reassuring. Most of Europe was then embroiled in the bloody wars of religion between Catholics and Protestants, and the Jesuits, who were men of peace in Japan, were active leaders of the warlike European Catholics. Perhaps even more disquieting was the arrival of the Spaniards in the Far East. The Portuguese usually confined themselves to peaceful trading, but the Spaniards were bent on conquest and did not conceal their intent. In 1575 they had conquered the island of Luzon in the Philippine Islands and built a powerful outpost at Manila. The Japanese knew all about this, since they had Philippine settlements of their own, and they very likely heard the Spaniards boasting—quite correctly—that Spanish military power was the terror of the Western world.

If Hideyoshi feared that the Christians, especially the well-armed and notoriously aggressive Spaniards, might form the nucleus of a league to overthrow him, he had grounds for his wariness. His expulsion order may simply have been intended as a warning to the Jesuits to keep out of Japanese politics; its enforcement was probably deliberately ignored, for fear of interfering with the valuable Portuguese trade passing through the Jesuit stronghold of Nagasaki.

In any case, the comparatively minor problem of the Christians was not uppermost in Hideyoshi's mind. He still had stubborn enemies in the eastern provinces and the far north. Working with his ally, Ieyasu, he collected a great army, and in April 1590 marched out of Kyoto at the head of a well-disciplined force of perhaps 200,000 men carrying the latest weapons.

The first objective of the campaign was in the east—the strongly fortified castle of Odawara, belonging to the powerful Hojo family, who were distantly connected with the Hojo rulers of early feudal times. Hideyoshi did not attack it head-on, which would have been a bloody business; he settled down to besiege it. While waiting for the defenders to be starved out, he wrote to his wife a touching letter that hints he was moved not only by sentiment but also by patriotism. "I long for the Young Lord [his little son Tsurumatsu]," he wrote, "but I must give up my longing. If we destroy Odawara the way is clear to Dewa and Mutsu. That means one-third of all Japan, and although I am getting old I must think of the future and what is best for the country."

He also asked his wife to send him his favourite concubine, Yodogimi, the mother of Tsurumatsu. For the entertainment of other besiegers, he rounded up local girls and brought dancers, musicians and courtesans from the capital. His officers were permitted to send for their wives, and merchants came from all over the country to keep them supplied with luxuries. These preparations for a long and comfortable siege were too much for the Hojo, who surrendered after a few months. Hideyoshi treated them rather generously, requiring only two of the leaders to kill themselves. The northern barons in Dewa and Mutsu submitted to him a little later. For the first time for more than 100 years Japan was at peace. For the first time, also, it was a united nation.

A MANY-ROOFED TOWER, *seen through the bars of a store-room window, is the charming but almost impregnable main defence of the White Heron.*

A
FEUDAL
LORD'S
FORTRESS
OF BEAUTY

The Japanese feudal lords of the late 16th and early 17th centuries needed sturdy, heavy-beamed castles to defend their tiny kingdoms in an almost continuous sequence of petty wars. Yet, true to tradition, their striving for security was matched by a concern for aesthetics. The castle exteriors were decorative, the grounds enhanced by flowering trees and still ponds.

Such a castle was the one at Himeji, called the White Heron because of its white plaster finish. Its 234 acres of land were crossed by heavy stone walls and labyrinthine paths designed to channel attackers towards bottleneck traps before they reached the main strongholds —four towers, or donjons. Situated on a hill-top, the castle dared warriors to storm it. But no one accepted the challenge, and today Himeji stands untouched, a relic of the day when feudal lords ruled the manor.

AN UPHILL COURSE TO THE CASTLE

No attackers ever laid siege to the White Heron castle; if they had, their task would have been a formidable one. The outer works began at the bottom of the hill; the donjon strongholds were at the crest (*top right*), the approach paths steep and beset with dangers. Attacking soldiers could be bombarded with rocks from above and swept by fusillades fired through holes in the walls.

The elaborate defences of the White Heron were justified by the strategic value of the site. Himeji controlled the link between western Japan and the capital city of Kyoto. In 1581 a future ruler of Japan named Hideyoshi built a small castle there. Legend has it that when the newly completed three-storey donjon began to lean, the chief mason climbed to the top of the tilting tower and threw himself off, a chisel wedged in his mouth, to restore his honour by suicide. The White Heron was completed in 1609 by a general of the powerful Tokugawa clan after workmen had toiled for nine years to make the fortress one of the loveliest and strongest castles in all Japan.

STRONGHOLDS TO REPEL THE ENEMY

A SECRET EXIT, *this gate needed no door, for it could be sealed with stones.*

For the White Heron to be captured, an army would have had to fight its way through no fewer than 11 gates that guarded the pathways between the lower entrance and the donjons.

The gates directly in the enemy's path were reinforced wooden barricades designed to halt an onslaught by their sheer bulk. The most difficult one to storm (*right*) was close to the main entrance of the donjons. Enemy troops who were funnelled towards this barrier had to make a 90-degree turn to approach it from the gate below; along the way they could be fired upon from wall-ports and windows and a near-by tower. If they breached the gate, defenders in a chamber above could remove floor boards and fire down on the attackers. Even if they won their way past this murderous line of defence, the assault troops would again have to make a sharp turn, climb a flight of stairs—and then find themselves confronting yet another stronghold.

AN IRON-PLATED DOOR *protected a main entrance; the small door permitted routine traffic to pass through whenever the large door was safely locked.*

A HALL TO ARM THE "RUNNING SOLDIERS"

The strongholds of the castle complex were the four donjons, which were interconnected by spacious, enclosed halls, each having a special military function. The biggest of these halls (*left*) was called the *musha bashiri*, which literally means "running soldiers". At the first threat of attack, the defending soldiers would run to this room to receive their weapons and be mustered into units. The racks between the windows on the right were intended to hold fire-arms, the dowels above the windows were for pikes.

This room, with its appointments, suggests a Japanese version of the stone keeps of medieval Europe. The resemblance is not entirely accidental. Japan's great era of castle building came after the Portuguese arrived with tales of European fortresses designed to resist attacking hordes. The Japanese, quick to take advantage of new ideas from abroad, may well have adapted the Portuguese suggestions to improve their own fortification.

THE PRINCESS'S APARTMENT (*above*), *its luxurious furniture now gone, was linked to the castle by a corridor (top) that once had polished wood floors.*

ROOMS FOR PLEASANT LIVING IN A STRONGHOLD

Life was relaxed and gay, if uneventful, at the White Heron. The 3,000 samurai stationed there were seldom engaged in battles, even though they kept the castle stripped for action in case an attack should come. The women of the castle, wives of the soldiers, enjoyed the easy routine of any peacetime military installation.

The lady of the castle from 1616 to 1626 was Princess Sen, for whose comfort a sumptuous apartment was added on to the castle (*below, left*). Here she presided over popular social activities, such as moon-viewing, which was accompanied by the sipping of *sake* and the reciting of poems. But when her husband died in 1626, she moved to a castle at Edo, and there, bored and distraught, she caused a minor scandal by waving the sleeves of her kimono from a window to attract the young men passing by. The families of later lords were less fortunate. The leaders of the ruling Tokugawa clans required the lord's wife and children to live apart from him at Edo as virtual hostages in case the lord revolted against Tokugawa authority.

A DOOR IN A DOOR *led to the women's area and was used whenever the big door was closed.*

HEAVY TRAP DOORS, *shown closed on the left, could be opened, as one is on the right, to give defenders access to floor ports for use against enemies below.*

BENEATH EVERY DECORATION, IRON SHIELDS

The architectural features of the castle, decorative as they might appear, always had a bearing on defence. No window was without bars, no outside wall without shooting holes, and even the balconies, such as the one below, served military as well as aesthetic functions. Placed at strategic points on the donjons, these balconies provided perches for soldiers firing guns or arrows between the bars. Should the enemy advance beneath them, trap doors in the floors could be raised (*left*) for stones to be dropped or boiling water poured down.

The materials used in the construction of these windows show how carefully the castle was conceived to blend the warlike and the beautiful. The bars were made entirely of wood and then covered by iron plating so that even an enemy who climbed up to the bars could not saw through them. But finally the functional iron plates were covered with a finish of white plaster, to make the windows harmonize with the all-white castle.

A GRACEFUL BALCONY, *which overhangs the wall, was equipped with large floor-openings through which missiles could be dropped on attackers.*

THE ORNATE TOWER THAT STOOD FOR FEUDALISM

The main donjon of the White Heron castle, with its many barred windows, sculpted tile roofs and scrollwork (*right*), symbolized the power of the feudal lord. Under attack, the donjon was the headquarters of the defence forces. In peacetime, it stood as a monument to authority; around it gathered nobles, peasants, merchants and soldiers to seek protection, do business and carry on the daily work.

The feudal power represented by the White Heron donjon did not slacken for nearly three centuries, while the castle passed through the hands of six families and 32 different masters. Then armed uprisings re-established imperial power, and feudalism ended in 1869. During this time of upheaval, the White Heron was fired on for the first time—a few token rifle shots that glanced off harmlessly. Today, the White Heron and scores of other castles are national monuments, preserved as memorials to the age of feudal lords.

8

A CLOSED JAPAN

The Japanese in the 17th century made another of their reversals of attitude towards foreigners. They slammed the door in the face of the outside world. For more than two centuries alien influences were kept out of Japan, while the Japanese were held inside their homeland. In their isolation they missed completely the intellectual, social and economic developments that transformed the West during this period. But they did not stagnate. They progressed on a course uniquely their own that would prepare them to slip readily into their modern role in world affairs.

This withdrawal into a state of seclusion, called the "Closed Country" by the Japanese, was a reaction to the influence of European religion, technology and ideas, which were considered a threat to the established order. It brought an abrupt end to a period of expansion that began in the 16th century. When Hideyoshi unified Japan in 1590, his country was interested in foreigners and sure of itself. So confident was Hideyoshi that he decided on a move unprecedented in Japanese history: large-scale foreign conquest.

Hideyoshi planned to invade and conquer China, a project that has been called a product of megalomania, but although it was certainly reckless it was by no means absurd. Japanese pirates and fighter-traders had easily won power and wealth in many far distant lands, and Hideyoshi may well have reasoned that if these small groups of his countrymen had had such remarkable success, his own large armies, now released from civil warfare, should be able to march to the ends of the earth. China may have looked to him like rather easy prey. Its Ming Dynasty was weakening, rotten with internal disorder and beset by nomadic tribes on its northern frontier. Indeed, it would soon be overthrown by one of those tribes, the Manchu, a people less advanced and less numerous than the Japanese, and no more warlike.

In May 1592, Hideyoshi's expeditionary force—some 150,000 men supplied with plenty of fire-arms—landed in Korea, then a Chinese tributary State, as the first stage of its march on the Ming capital at Peking. The Chinese at first did nothing. The Koreans resisted but soon collapsed, and Hideyoshi's generals plunged forward. Their armies swept up the peninsula with little opposition; one of them took Seoul and later Pyongyang, now the capital of North Korea, and chased the king of Korea to the river Yalu where he pleaded for help from China. At last the Chinese pulled themselves together (as they were to do in 1950 when the American general Douglas MacArthur also reached the Yalu in an over-extended condition), mustered a large army and forced the Japanese back down the peninsula. In 1597 there was a second invasion, but the Japanese never regained their momentum and eventually withdrew.

While Hideyoshi was preoccupied with his Chinese adventure, the Jesuit missionaries in Japan enjoyed a respite from the repressions initiated earlier. The edict of 1587 ordering their expulsion was not enforced; native converts were seldom disturbed, and they continued to grow rapidly in numbers and influence. But the Jesuits ran into trouble from quite another quarter: persistent efforts by the rival order of Franciscan friars to enter Japan from the Spanish-occupied Philippines. The Spanish Franciscans did not follow the same policy as the predominantly Portuguese Jesuits; instead of Christianizing a country by first converting the upper classes, they believed in mass evangelization with emotional appeals to crowds of commoners in the streets. The Jesuits feared that these aggressive, revolutionary tactics would rouse the opposition of Japanese authorities.

In spite of Jesuit attempts to keep the Franciscans out, a few arrived in 1593 and got an apparently friendly reception from Hideyoshi. They were delighted with Japan; more of them came from Manila and acted as if no expulsion edict had ever been issued. For a few years their aggressive proselytizing aroused no special antagonism among the Japanese, but in 1596 a great Spanish galleon from Manila was driven ashore on the island of Shikoku. Her rich cargo was claimed by both the samurai of Shikoku and Hideyoshi's local representatives, and in the ensuing dispute one of the ship's officers made a monumental strategic error. He threatened that if the cargo were not returned to him, the king of Spain would conquer Japan. Unhappily, he also mentioned the Spanish custom of using missionary friars to pave the way for Spanish conquest.

These remarks were repeated to Hideyoshi, who reacted quickly by condemning the Franciscans to crucifixion. On the 5th February 1597, the savage sentence was carried out. Six Franciscans, seventeen of their Japanese friars-in-training and three Japanese Jesuit lay brothers (included by mistake) were crucified at Nagasaki. For a while it looked as if Hideyoshi, having suppressed the Franciscans, intended to eliminate Christianity altogether, but the persecution slackened, probably because he still considered the Jesuits necessary for promoting trade by way of Portuguese ships. In the next year, 1598, he died and the Christians got another respite.

Hideyoshi's successor was Tokugawa Ieyasu, his old ally and his deputy in the eastern provinces of Honshu. Ieyasu moved smoothly into Hideyoshi's place by dominating a council of regency that had been created to govern in the name of Hideyoshi's five-year-old son, whom Ieyasu later deposed. The inevitable rebellion of barons came almost immediately, but Ieyasu was victorious in the Battle of Sekigahara in 1600, and the emperor made him shogun in 1603, when he was 61 years old. So began the Tokugawa shogunate that was to rule Japan for 264 years, until 1867.

During the early years of his régime, Ieyasu was tolerant of Christianity if not actually favourable towards it. Like Hideyoshi, he was eager for European knowledge and trade and feared that the flow of both would be cut off if he persecuted the Jesuit. But events in Europe were soon to change

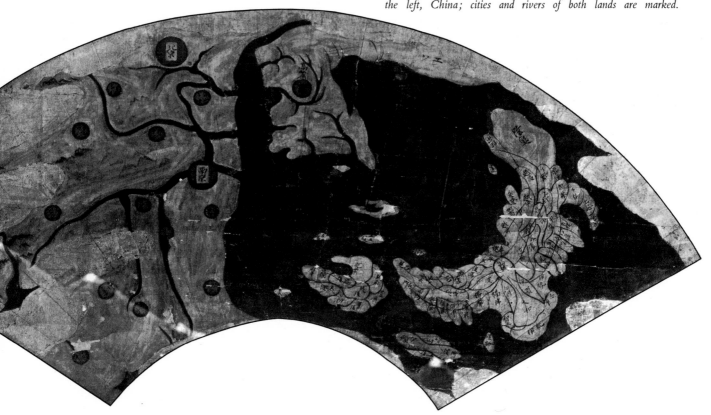

his attitude. For some years the vigorous Protestant Dutch had been defying the sea power of Catholic Spain and Portugal, and in 1600 the first Dutch ship, the *Liefde*, put into Beppu Bay in Kyushu. When the Jesuits in Nagasaki heard that the heretical Dutch were only a few miles away, they allegedly urged the Japanese authorities to crucify the Protestants as pirates. The local daimyo was not in a crucifying mood; he gave the "Red Hairs" (as the Japanese called the Dutch) full hospitality, and Ieyasu invited the *Liefde*'s pilot, an Englishman named Will Adams, to visit him. This was a setback for the Jesuits. Adams gave Ieyasu the first Protestant account of the bloody religious wars that were devastating Europe and no doubt stressed the militant part played in them by the European Jesuits. It was not a pretty

picture, and it must have made Ieyasu think hard about the Christian minority that was growing so fast in Japan.

Ieyasu was much impressed with Will Adams and made him a close adviser. More Dutch arrived and were granted the right to establish a trading post at Hirado in Kyushu. Whenever Adams or the Dutch got a chance, they pointed out to influential Japanese that in case of an uprising against the shogun, the Jesuits' converts, many of whom were warriors, could hold a good part of Kyushu until Spanish soldiers and weapons from Manila had time to arrive by sea.

Ieyasu had heard all this from the Buddhists, but now he began to listen more carefully. In Japanese eyes the missionaries had recently changed for the worse. The aggressive Franciscans, temporarily suppressed by Hideyoshi, had returned, and their conspicuous methods of proselytizing alarmed the authorities, who wanted least of all a popular religious upheaval under foreign control.

In the early 1600's there were probably 300,000 Christians in Japan, and they seemed to be coalescing into a tight minority that valued its religion above everything else. This sectarian partisanship, which cut across feudal lines of loyalty, seemed to Ieyasu a serious threat to his régime. He saw another threat in the dreaded Spaniards who were increasingly in evidence. In 1611–1612, a Spanish navigator, Sebastián Vizcaíno, made a hydrographic survey along the east coast of Japan. When Ieyasu asked Will Adams what he thought about it, Adams answered that in Europe such activities were considered preliminary to an invasion. He had probably already told Ieyasu about the great Spanish Armada that had attempted to conquer his own island country, England, in 1588.

Ieyasu made up his mind slowly, apparently weighing the threat of the growing Christian minority against the benefit of the European trade and contacts that had been associated in his mind with the missionaries. A strong new factor in his reasoning was his conviction that the Protestant Dutch and the English, whose first ship reached Japan in 1613, would continue to trade even if all the Catholic missionaries were expelled.

In 1613, a crowd of 30,000 Christians gathered to pray and sing hymns at the execution of several co-religionists. When the news reached Ieyasu he decided to eliminate Japanese Christianity. He decreed that all missionaries must leave the country; all Japanese Christians must join some Buddhist sect and convince Buddhist priests that they had really changed their faith.

Unlike Hideyoshi's anti-Christian decrees, this one was enforced, though not hurriedly. Most of the foreign missionaries were concentrated at Na-

gasaki, where more than 90 of them took Portuguese ships out of the country. A smaller number hid or disguised themselves thinly as foreign merchants. For a few years the Japanese Christians were not actively persecuted; Ieyasu apparently believed that they were not dangerous without their foreign leaders, and observed with pleasure that after the missionaries had departed or gone underground, foreign trade was hardly affected. Even the pious Portuguese kept on visiting Nagasaki.

Ieyasu died in 1616 at the age of 74 and was succeeded in power by his son, Hidetada, who was harder on the Christians. Four clandestine missionaries were caught and beheaded in 1617, and native Christians who refused to recant began to be executed in considerable numbers.

The attack on Christianity was only part of a broader movement in Japan. As familiarity with the outside world increased, the intellectual climate of the country—or at least of its leaders—was becoming more and more hostile to foreign influences, secular as well as religious. Japanese who had journeyed to Europe brought back alarming reports. Europe, with its warlike religious factions, its powerful weapons and its clashing political ideas, was an obvious threat to the feudal system dominated by the shogun and his advisers.

Apparently no Japanese of the time realized that the cause of Europe's turmoil—and the source of its great vitality—was an intellectual awakening of overpowering significance. Since most of their information had come through missionaries whose church was largely anti-scientific, the Japanese got only the haziest notion of the scientific and technical revolution that was sweeping Renaissance Europe and would soon give its comparatively small countries control over much of the earth.

Perhaps the three great unifiers of Japan—Nobunaga, Hideyoshi and Ieyasu—would have understood this portentous truth if it had been fairly presented to them. They were all intelligent and venturesome men, and open to new ideas. Japan in the early 17th century was not behind Europe in most respects, and its prompt adoption of fire-arms showed how quickly it could master a new and useful European technique. If the political cli-mate had been favourable, Japan's technology might have caught up with Europe's in the 17th century as effectively as it did in the 19th, when the gap between them was much wider. If that had hap-pened, Japan might well have become a great colonial power controlling much of East Asia.

But Hidetada and the later Tokugawa shogun had no such vision. Their overriding purpose was to preserve their own position at the apex of the feudal pyramid. Any influence from outside they saw as a threat to this rigid political structure. Christianity was such an influence, and so when the comparatively moderate Hidetada retired as shogun in 1623 and was succeeded by his son Ie-mitsu, there began a period of persecution in which thousands of Christians were martyred.

Much has been written about this savage period, but it must be remembered that Japan was not the only 17th-century country where men and women were forced to die painfully for their reli-gion. In Europe the Spanish Inquisition was routinely burning thousands of heretics. The Thir-ty Years' War, essentially a conflict between Catholics and Protestants, was already raging and would quickly reduce parts of Central Europe to cannibalism. No Westerner can justly condemn Japan for its share of the horrors of the age.

In 1633 the shogunate began to issue a series of edicts, the Exclusion Decrees, whose aim was to break almost completely Japan's contacts with the outside world. Japanese subjects were for-bidden to go abroad or to build ships capable of ocean voyages. Those who had been living abroad for more than a specified length of time, and had

presumably been corrupted, were forbidden to come home under pain of death.

A bloody rebellion of thousands of Christian peasants near Nagasaki in 1637 accelerated Japan's policy of withdrawal. After the revolt was cruelly stamped out, the government exiled the Portuguese merchants, who were believed to be implicated in the revolt, and forbade them to re-enter Japan. When a Portuguese ship brought a mission to Na-gasaki to plead for reconsideration, the Japanese executed all the envoys and most of the ship's crew, a total of 61 persons.

After this emphatic gesture Japan was almost to-tally shut off from the world. Contact with dangerous Europe was limited to one or two Dutch ships licensed each year to visit Nagasaki. All Europeans were expelled from the country ex-cept for a handful of Dutch merchants confined to a small island in Nagasaki harbour. Besides for-eign goods, the Dutch ships brought a trickle of Western knowledge, but it had hardly any effect. For more than two centuries, while the Western world passed through the rapid evolution of the in-dustrial revolution, Japan elaborated in seclusion its pre-industrial culture.

The basic policy of the Tokugawa shogunate was to preserve Japan's traditional type of military feudalism, and to perpetuate its own power. In concentrating on these objectives, the shogunate buttressed its position with rules and requirements that strongly suggest the machinery of a modern police State. No one in Japan was supposed to go unwatched, no one was supposed to change his level in life.

One important step towards ensuring the power of the Tokugawa, however, was an innovation of Ieyasu, founder of the line. In the early 1600's, he had moved the shogunate headquarters from Kyoto to Edo (now Tokyo), an easily defensible site in

ODA NOBUNAGA

TOYOTOMI HIDEYOSHI

TOKUGAWA IEYASU

the rich eastern provinces. This was probably a conscious return to the policy of Japan's first shogun, who, more than 300 years earlier, had made his headquarters in the eastern provinces to avoid the intrigues and softening culture of the emperor's capital, Kyoto. The emperor and his courtiers stayed in Kyoto where Ieyasu supported them in modest affluence, and watchful officials made sure that none of the emperor's circle had any contact with potentially dangerous daimyo.

For a while the static society enforced by the Tokugawa was stable and successful. The lordly daimyo were still rich, but some of them were hardly more than bureaucrats. Others, who had submitted to Ieyasu only after he had won control in the Battle of Sekigahara, were known as "Outside Lords" and were carefully watched by the shogun's officials. Their marriages and successions were supervised. They were forbidden to improve or repair their castles without the shogun's permission, but when the shogun wanted to build a castle, he called on the Outside Lords for large amounts of money. If the expenditure made them poor, so much the better. They were the less likely to start trouble.

Perhaps the greatest burden on the more important daimyo—and the most effective restraint on their rebelliousness—was the requirement that they spend part of each alternate year in Edo and leave their wives and heirs there as hostages whenever they visited their fiefs. Their journeys to and from Edo, accompanied by throngs of servants and retainers, come to be colourful processions, but extremely expensive ones. All roads leading to Edo were "sword and women" check points, where guards watched for any illegal weapons being smuggled into the capital and for the families of daimyo being smuggled out. Either was considered an indication of intended rebellion.

The classes below the daimyo were closely

THE FAMILY CRESTS *of the three men who unified Japan in the 16th and 17th centuries—Nobunaga, Hideyoshi and Ieyasu—are stylized depictions of flowers and leaves. Originally a crest, or "mon", could be worn only by a noble; later, samurai also used crests. During the Tokugawa period Kabuki actors and other commoners devised "mon" for their families and wore them on their kimonos.*

watched also. The proud samurai were no longer country gentlemen living on their own estates and ready to spring to arms at their lord's command. The higher ranks were bureaucrats or the equivalent of army officers. The lower ranks were soldiers. Almost all of them lived on salaries paid by the daimyo. Their weapons were provided for them and their movements and activities were closely restricted. Nevertheless they enjoyed some startling advantages over the commoners. If a samurai felt, for instance, that he had been insulted by a person of low birth, he could cut him in two with his sword and suffer no punishment. This privilege, which was not exercised frequently, was called "permission to cut down and leave".

As the Tokugawa régime hardened, the peasants, who were the bulk of the population, lost almost all their rights. Tax collectors took about half of their crops and tried to leave barely enough to keep the cultivators alive and at work. The most fortunate commoners were the townsmen. Skilled artisans earned a fairly good living, and merchants and money lenders grew rich in spite of government efforts to restrict their activities.

This archaic social structure did not remain unmodified for long. Even with Japan secluded from the world, the forces of change were too strong to be checked by the rather fumbling measures of the shogunate. For one thing, the towns and cities were growing fast, and the complicated activities and interests of their inhabitants did not fit into the feudal fabric of lords, soldiers and peasants. Edo grew fastest of all. When Ieyasu made it the capital of the shogunate, it was no more than a village, but in 1700, about a century later, its population was something like 500,000. Those daimyo who were required to spend part of their lives in Edo vied with each other in building their elaborate palaces and staffing them with swarms of retainers, and their demand for luxuries

attracted skilled workers from all over the country.

The shogun certainly had not foreseen this disquieting result of their policy of making the daimyo live at Edo, and they could do little about it except issue endless decrees urging the townspeople to return to ancient simplicity. Another thing they could not control was money and finance. Japan had used coinage to some extent for many centuries, but it also used a barter system based on rice, the unit being the *koku*, the amount of rice (about five bushels) that an average Japanese ate in a year. Since rice would be exchanged for other things, this barter economy worked fairly well when food was consumed by the people who raised it and by others near by. But to keep large cities supplied with food and manufactured goods brought from a distance required a less cumbersome medium. By 1600 gold and silver coins were in wide use; by 1700 Japan had a full money economy using a great variety of coins.

The people who understood money and the associated mysteries of money-changing, credit and finance were not the daimyo or samurai, who were essentially warriors, uneducated in the ways of commerce. Money was the familiar tool of the city-dwelling merchants, and soon they were using it to concentrate in their own hands a large part of the national wealth. They grew rich speculating in rice, whose price fluctuated violently. And they multiplied their capital by lending money to the daimyo, who were passionately fond of display and often short of cash to underwrite it. A contemporary author estimated that around 1700 the debts of the daimyo were one hundred times as great as all the money in the country.

The townsmen's affluence put them in an equivocal position. Traditionally merchants, bankers, speculators and other people who made their living by trading instead of by producing were accorded low social rank. The shogunate frequently warned prosperous townsmen not to imitate their social betters. They should dress plainly, it told them, and never give lavish entertainments. The rich merchants and bankers, of course, did no such thing, and they usually had enough purse-power to evade official coercion. About their only concession was the clothing they wore in public; often it was ostensibly plain—but the linings of their outer robes and the garments worn under them might be bright brocade.

Towards the end of the 17th century, a brilliant and rather raffish culture developed in the thriving cities. While the aristocracy clung to older arts and entertainments—traditional music, the formal *No* plays and the restrained eloquence of the tea ceremony—the townsfolk demanded lusty pleasures. These they found in what was called the Floating World of restaurants and theatres, prostitutes and bath-girls, wrestlers, singers and dancers. It was a world whose colourful life may be glimpsed in surviving popular novels of the times, many of them highly erotic, and in wood-block prints illustrating the vivid life of the big cities.

One of the permanent achievements of the Floating World was Kabuki, a form of popular drama, which still has great appeal in modern Japan and which preserves traditions established centuries ago. The audiences of early Kabuki theatres included many wives and daughters of the merchant class who found in the performances, and sometimes in the actors, a way of escape from their dull, subordinated lives.

The shogunate disapproved of the Floating World and of the townsmen who supported it. Sometimes a merchant or banker would make too great a display of wealth, and the shogun would summarily confiscate everything he had. This did not happen very often, for it came to be tacitly accepted that within the licensed entertainment districts of the cities the old rules of social class did not apply. In the Floating World, a townsman could show off his wealth whenever and however he felt like it.

Some of the townsmen acquired samurai rank, most often by paying a debt-ridden samurai to adopt them into his family. Changes of social relationship were felt even in the villages, where enterprising peasants organized small businesses and freed themselves from feudal bondage.

For more than a century after 1638 practically no European ideas entered the Closed Country, and not until the West reappeared did interest in them revive. Indeed, some European techniques, such as the manufacture and use of fire-arms, were largely eliminated to preserve the prestige of samurai swordsmanship. But nevertheless Japan kept pace with the Western world in its own fashion. Education spread to all classes. It is estimated that before 1850, while Japan was still "closed", perhaps 40 per cent of Japanese males were literate, a proportion that most European countries of the time could not match.

Though the power-driven machines and the scientific methods of thought that produced industrialism were wholly lacking, Japanese artisans were as highly skilled as any on earth and capable of quickly learning new techniques. Japanese commerce and banking were elaborate and flexible and easy to mesh with Western practices.

When, in 1853, the Black Ships of the American Commodore Matthew Perry steamed into Edo Bay and forced Japan to reopen the closed country after 214 years of nearly total seclusion, Japan was not an "undeveloped" land. It was highly advanced, a nation whose last two centuries of development had followed non-Western lines. So it "caught up" with the West with remarkable ease while preserving for the world's pleasure the greater part of its distinctive culture.

KABUKI—A THEATRE OF ESCAPISM

At the beginning of the 17th century, Japan closed its doors to the world and became a rigid, isolated country; paradoxically, this same period saw the birth of Kabuki, an extremely colourful and melodramatic form of theatre. While the rulers of Japan were enforcing a stultifying political *status quo*, the people were flocking to bright, bizarre spectacles. Most Kabuki patrons were merchants, who were forbidden by the government to wear sumptuous clothes or even change professions. Starved for excitement and lavish display, they were dazzled by the Kabuki's resplendent costumes, such as the one worn by the courtesan pictured above. The audiences delighted even more in scenes that presented clever commoners outwitting their social superiors in love or physical combat. In fact, a battle between a young commoner and a samurai bully is the subject of one of the Kabuki's most famous and enduring plays, *Sukeroku*, a melodramatic work that is still performed in the traditional manner.

Photographs by Norman Snyder

The strange conventions of a theatrical tradition based on music,

Although a few Kabuki plays dealt with very realistic and topical problems, the productions were extremely stylized and tradition-bound. Kabuki was derived from an ancient form of popular dance, and some Kabuki plays were interrupted by dance interludes. Kabuki's dance origins were also recalled by the rhythmic way actors moved and grouped themselves in symmetrical compositions, like the one formed by courtesans and their attendants shown on the right, above. Similarly, when minor characters, like the courtesans on the right, below, are not involved in the action, they are grouped so that they will focus the audience's attention towards the centre of interest.

Another departure from realism was the use of men to play women's parts. Actresses were banned from the Kabuki stage in 1629, when the government discovered that many women were doubling off-stage as prostitutes and their performances were highly suggestive; the government feared the actresses were causing a decline in public morals.

The one place where the classes could mingle freely was in the courtesans' section of each city, and a house in Edo's licensed quarter is shown in the one set of *Sukeroku*. There a courtesan named Agemaki reigns supreme (*top, left*) and the play involves the rivalry over her between Sukeroku, a commoner (*centre*) and Ikyu, an old, villainous samurai (*bottom*).

ncing and stylized acting.

Sukeroku, the hero of the play of the same name, enters and jauntily twirls an umbrella. His custume establishes him as an "otoko-date", or a man ready to defend the lower classes against bullying warriors. Only a samurai could wear two swords; Sukeroku reveals, by carrying one sword, that he is in a social position somewhere between the commoner's and the samurai's. That he is at odds with the established order of society is suggested by his purple head-band; this colour was customarily worn only by the shogun.

The entrance of the hero — an impressive display of courage, manly grace and wild bravado

Ikyu, infuriated by Sukeroku's impertinence, reaches for his sword—but stops himself. He does not draw his sword because it is a stolen one, a precious heirloom called Tomokirimaru, which rightfully belonged to Sukeroku's family. Ikyu, realizing that he has been insulted to provoke him into betraying his theft, now smothers his rage.

After his dance Sukeroku lounges on a bench before the admiring eyes of the courtesans. When the villain of the play, a samurai named Ikyu, envies the attention Sukeroku is receiving and seeks similar courtesies, Sukeroku incites his enemy's anger with a contemptuous rebuff: he offers Ikyu a pipe, ordinarily a polite gesture—but insolently presents it held between his toes.

The heroine: Agemaki, a courtesan whose beauty and refinement have won her the love of Sukeroku

Alone with his sweetheart, the courtesan Agemaki, Sukeroku assures her of his undy[ing]
love, which she returns. The fact that Agemaki is a courtesan does not detract from her [de]-
sirability in Sukeroku's eyes. For most Japanese men, marriages were arranged by paren[ts];
the men, therefore, often turned to courtesans for the love they could not find at ho[me].

Carried away by his rage, Ikyu strikes Sukeroku with his fan. The fan is the most frequently used stage prop in Kabuki, and, depending on how it is moved, can be employed to express a host of emotions, as well as to stand for such objects as a sword, chopsticks, fluttering leaves, wind or waves.

Ikyu enters and tries to make love to Agemaki, unaware that Sukeroku has hidden under her skirts. The heavy folds of her costume conceal him easily, since it consists of many layers of kimonos and a huge sash, or obi. From this hiding place, Sukeroku provokes Ikyu. Every time Ikyu draws near the girl, Sukeroku mutters an insult (top) or pinches Ikyu's legs. At last Sukeroku emerges from his mistress's skirts (bottom) and confronts his enemy.

175

As the argument becomes more heated, Ikyu forgets his resolve not to draw his sword in Sukeroku's presence, and pulls it out of its scabbard. He aims a blow at a three-legged incense burner near him and cuts it in half. Sukeroku looks at the sword—and sees that it is his family's heirloom, Tomokirimaru. This dramatic moment is held for a moment as the actors freeze into a tableau. Frozen poses are often assumed by Kabuki actors to emphasize a crucial turning-point of the plot, and directors compose them carefully so that they form memorable visual images tense with contained energy.

A duel between Sukeroku and Ikyu has become inevitable now that Sukeroku knows that Ikyu is the man who stole the family heirloom sword. The two combatants strip down to the white kimonos they ordinarily wear as undergarments, and Ikyu's retainer ceremoniously presents them with swords. In the ensuing conflict, Ikyu wounds Sukeroku in the shoulder, and Sukeroku falls to the ground, feigning death. The entire scene is more like a dance than a duel; each thrust and parry is choreographed with precision and performed in slow motion.

Believing that Sukeroku is dead or dying, Ikyu prepares to deliver the coup de grace (right). Sukeroku, however, avoids the blow, throws Ikyu off balance, hurls him to the ground and slays him (below). Now Sukeroku has not only recovered his family sword, but he has also obtained revenge. Such a dramatic moment represents not necessarily a climax for the Japanese audiences. The Japanese do not go to the Kabuki theatre in order to witness a suspenseful plot or a deep psychological study of a character. Attending a play is as much a social event as an artistic experience; ordinarily the Kabuki theatre is a beehive of activity as the audience eats and chats. Most of the plots are well known and often a programme consists of one act from one play, another act from a different work, and so on. The real appeal of Kabuki lies in the actor's skill, particularly his skill in assuming a beautiful and forceful pose, which in Kabuki terminology is called a "mie". If a "mie" proves to be unusually striking, the audience will shout in approval, "This is what I've been waiting for!"

The closing moments of the play: the hero's narrow escape and happy reunion with his brave mistres

In the last scene of the play, Sukeroku hea the shouts of an angry crowd that has learn of Ikyu's death and is coming to avenge hi Seeking to hide from the crowd, Sukeroku co ceals himself in a huge wooden tub—whi contains real water. Such a realistic effect u rare for Kabuki, though playwrights did occ sionally delight their audiences with flashy scen of this sort. Kabuki theatres had trap doors ar after 1758, revolving stages that were turn from below by stage hands; this equiment u used for quick set changes, sudden appearanc of ghosts, convincing depictions of trees falli and mansions collapsing in violent earthquak Other devices were employed to whisk acto through the air and to create strange optical a sound effects. Butterflies and birds were flou in on slender poles and costumed actors pranc about the stage as bears, horses and lior

Emerging from the water, Sukeroku holds his wounded shoulder (left), staggers a few paces and collapses in a faint. Luckily, just before the return of the mob, which is still hunting for him, Agemaki discovers him and conceals him once again under her skirts. After she sends the crowd off in a wrong direction (below), Agemaki revives her lover. He promises to meet her that evening in the fields outside town; then he climbs a rope ladder and escapes across roof-tops to freedom —and presumably to a life of happiness in another city with his beloved mistress, Agemaki.

CROSS-ROAD CIVILIZATIONS BETWEEN EAST AND WEST

The chart on the right is designed to show the duration of early Japanese civilization, and to relate it to others in the "Crossroad" group of cultures that are considered in one major group of volumes in this series. Examination of this chart will enable the reader to relate Japan's early culture to important cultural periods in other parts of the Far East and to Western exploration and colonization.

On the following pages is a chronological listing of important events that took place in the period covered by this book.

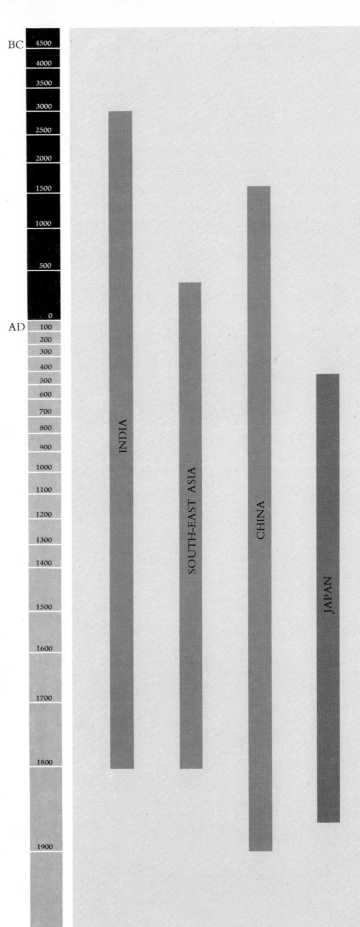

CHRONOLOGY—*A listing of significant events in the history of Early Japan*

	Politics and Warfare	PERIOD	Arts and Religion	
B.C.	Jimmu Tenno, semi-legendary emperor claiming descent from the Sun Goddess, is traditional founder of the Imperial Family in 660 B.C.	ARCHAIC	Wet method of rice culture, cloth weaving, and smelting and forging of iron are introduced from mainland Asia during second and first centuries B.C.	B.C.
A.D.	A Chinese traveller reports in A.D. 238 that Wa (Japan) consists of petty States ruled by women Mongoloid invaders arrive from Asia around A.D. 250 and soon establish themselves as aristocracy of Japan Japanese State expands from Kyushu to Yamoto region on the island of Honshu		Early Japanese religion grows probably as a form of nature-worship	A.D.
c. 500	Soga family wins control of the Imperial Court In A.D. 552 Chinese civilization begins to have marked influence on Japan Prince Shotoku is named heir-apparent to the throne by Umako, the Soga high minister, in A.D. 593 The so-called first constitution of Japan is formulated in A.D. 604 by Prince Shotoku Soga family is driven from power during a period of civil warfare Emperor Kotoku ascends the throne; the Fujiwara family begins its rise to dominance The Taika Reform decrees, designed to strengthen the central government, are issued by Emperor Kotoku	EARLY HISTORIC	Chinese script is adopted for official purposes around the beginning of fifth century; written records are kept for the first time King of Paikche in Korea sends a bronze Buddha and Buddhist scriptures to Japanese Court, spurring great interest in Buddhism, which becomes principal carrier of Chinese culture Ministers of the Soga family encourage building of Buddhist monasteries and temples and the assimilation of Chinese cultural ideas The Horyuji monastery is founded by the Imperial Family in A.D. 607; its Golden Hall is believed to be the world's oldest existing wooden building	c. 500
710	Nara, Japan's first permanent capital, is founded in A.D. 710 Dokyo, a scheming Buddhist monk with great influence over the Empress Koken, unsuccessfully plots to upset the throne and become emperor Kammu becomes emperor of Japan and in A.D. 784 moves the capital from Nara to Nagaoka	NARA	Buddhism and Shinto are reconciled around A.D. 740 and Buddhism becomes the Court religion; in A.D. 749 a colossal image of the Buddha is consecrated in Nara	710
794	A new capital, Heian-kyo, is founded by Emperor Kammu in A.D. 794 on the site of present-day Kyoto Following the return of a Japanese embassy in A.D. 838, communication with China is largely broken off because of disorderly conditions within the T'ang Empire The power and affluence of Japan's central government begins to deteriorate by the start of the 11th century, as provincial barons increase their independence The powerful Taira and Minamoto families help the Fujiwara-dominated government to maintain law and order in the provinces and suppress pirates in the Inland Sea Emperor Go Sanjo comes to the throne in 1068 and checks the power of the Fujiwara; he abdicates in favour of his son Shirakawa but continues to govern as Retired Emperor The Minamoto family gains strong influence at Court, leading to a power struggle between the Minamoto and Taira factions; warfare erupts in Kyoto In 1160 the Taira leader Kiyomori seizes control of the central government	HEIAN	Although direct contacts with China are broken off, Japanese art, architecture and literature continue to follow Chinese patterns, with Japanese innovations The aristocracy places great emphasis on elaborate manners and on such arts as calligraphy, poetry and perfume-blending *Kana,* or syllabic writing, comes into wide use by women in writing poems, letters, diaries and novels *The Tale of Genji,* the world's first novel, is written by Lady Murasaki Shikibu around 1020 Honen, a Buddhist monk, forms the *Jodo,* or Pure Land, sect in 1175 and begins to spread the worship of the Buddha Amida	794
1185	The Minamoto faction under Yoritomo crushes the Taira in 1185 Minamoto Yoritomo begins to build a government based on the samurai's feudal code of loyalty and service; he appoints loyal vassals to high offices Kamakura becomes headquarters for Yoritomo's military dictatorship Yoritomo is named first shogun of Japan in 1192	KAMAKU	The rise of the warrior caste stimulates improvements in sword-making; Japanese swords become the world's finest *The Tales of the Heike,* and other Kamakura war tales glorifying the deeds of warriors, gain wide popularity	1185

ASHIKAGA

1338

...after an inconclusive battle the invaders' ships are dispersed by a storm

A second Mongol invasion of Japan is attempted in 1281, but fails when a typhoon wrecks the Mongol fleets

Ashikaga Takauji, a Hojo general, defects to the Emperor Go Daigo in 1333; the Hojo regency ends and Kamakura is burned in a civil war

Ashikaga Takauji replaces Go Daigo with a puppet emperor and rules from Kyoto; Go Daigo establishes a rival Court south of the capital

Ashikaga Takauji becomes shogun in 1338, but warfare between the two rival Courts continues for about 50 years

Trade and diplomatic exchanges with China increase after Ashikaga Yoshimitsu becomes shogun in 1367; he suppresses the Japanese pirates who have been raiding the northern coasts of China

Government becomes increasingly chaotic under the shogun following Yoshimitsu; Japan begins to break up into many semi-independent principalities ruled by daimyo

Peasants revolt against government officials and invade Kyoto in defiance of the shogunate

Yoshimasa becomes shogun in 1449, but is a notably ineffective ruler

The Onin civil war breaks out in 1467; the central government collapses and the Imperial Family is impoverished

The Onin War ends in 1477, but fighting continues in the provinces

Kyoto revives as a great cultural centre, now under strong Zen influence; Ashikaga shoguns build palaces in the Muromachi quarter and patronize the arts

The No theatre develops from popular entertainments into a sophisticated form of drama

In 1394 Ashikaga Yoshimitsu builds the Golden Pavilion and lays out its garden

The Silver Pavilion is built by Ashikaga Yoshimasa in 1479; in its tea-room Yoshimasa and his guests elaborate the ritual of the tea ceremony

Sesshu perfects the Japanese technique of ink painting, reflecting in his work Zen principles of simplicity and restraint

COUNTRY AT WAR

1500

By 1500 all Japan is wracked by civil war

Japanese pirates start to make permanent trading settlements in South-East Asia

The Portuguese arrive in Japan c. 1542 and introduce fire-arms

Nobunaga defeats an army of the powerful daimyo Imagawa in 1560 and becomes a national figure

Nobunaga occupies Kyoto in 1568 and dominates central Japan

Nobunaga declares war on Buddhist sects, destroying monasteries and the religious centre at Mt. Hiei

Nobunaga demonstrates the superiority of fire-arms at the Battle of Nagashino, 1575

Hideyoshi succeeds to Nobunaga's power in 1582; he formulates repressive laws aimed at freezing Japan into a rigid feudal pattern

Hideyoshi subdues the last of his adversaries in 1590 and rules a united Japan

In 1592 Hideyoshi launches an unsuccessful invasion of China

Tokugawa Ieyasu succeeds Hideyoshi in 1598, defeats rebellious daimyo at Battle of Sekigahara and emerges as master of Japan; he moves the shogunate headquarters from Kyoto to Edo (now Tokyo)

A Jesuit mission headed by St. Francis Xavier lands in Japan in 1549 and is given permission to preach Christianity and make converts

Nagasaki becomes the Jesuits' headquarters, as well as a terminal for Portuguese trading ships

During the rule of Hideyoshi, the flowering of flamboyant Momoyama art and architecture reflects a diminishing interest in Zen's austere aesthetic principles

Hideyoshi orders the Jesuit missionaries expelled from Japan in 1587, but the expulsion order is not enforced

Franciscan missionaries arrive in Japan from the Spanish-occupied Philippines

In 1597 Hideyoshi executes six Franciscans and some of their followers and destroys a number of churches

TOKUGAWA

1603

Tokugawa Ieyasu is appointed shogun in 1603

Hidetada succeeds to Ieyasu's power in 1616 and is succeeded in turn by his son Iemitsu

Hostility to foreign secular and religious influences increases; these are seen as a threat to the rigid social structure maintained by the shogunate

Decrees of Shogun Iemitsu prohibit Japanese from travelling out of the country

The Portuguese are expelled in 1639 on suspicion of being implicated in a revolt by Christian peasants; except for a few Dutch merchants, all other Europeans are soon excluded

Tukugawa Ieyasu orders all missionaries to leave Japan; many leave, others go into hiding

Shogun Iemitsu institutes a period of intense persecution during which thousands of Japanese Christians are martyred

Japanese culture develops in isolation, including such art forms as the Kabuki theatre

BIBLIOGRAPHY

The following volumes were selected during the preparation of this book for their interest and authority, and for their usefulness to readers seeking additional information on spe-cific points. An asterisk (★) marks works available in both hardcover and paperback editions; a dagger (†) indicates availability only in paperback.

GENERAL HISTORY

Boxer, C. R., *The Christian Century in Japan, 1549-1650.* Rev. ed. University of California Press, 1967.
Boxer, C. R., ed., *A True Description of the Mighty Kingdoms of Japan and Siam, by François Caron and Joost Schouten.* Argonaut, 1935.
Cipolla, Carlo M., *Guns, Sails and Empires.*★ Funk & Wagnalls, 1967.
Cooper, Michael, S. J., ed., *They Came to Japan; An Anthology of European Reports on Japan, 1543–1640.* University of California Press, 1965.
Cressey, George B., *Asia's Lands and Peoples.* 3rd ed. McGraw-Hill, 1963.
Hall, John Whitney, *Government and Local Power in Japan, 500 to 1700.* Princeton University Press, 1966.
Hall, John W., and Richard K. Beardsley, *Twelve Doors to Japan.* McGraw-Hill, 1965
Keene, Donald, *Japanese Discovery of Europe.* Grove, 1954.
Murdoch, James, *History of Japan.* 3 vols. Frederick Ungar, 1964.
Reischauer, Edwin O., *Japan, Past and Present.* 3rd rev. ed. Alfred A. Knopf, 1964.
Reischauer, Edwin O., and John K. Fairbank, *East Asia: The Great Tradition.* Houghton Mifflin, 1960.
Sansom, George B.:
    History of Japan. 3 vols. Stanford University Press, 1958–1963.
    Japan, A Short Cultural History. Rev. ed. Appleton-Century-Crofts, 1962.
    The Western World and Japan. Alfred A. Knopf, 1965.
Varley, H. Paul, *The Onin War.* Columbia University Press, 1967.

RELIGION AND PHILOSOPHY

Anesaki Masaharu, *History of Japanese Religion.* Charles E. Tuttle, 1963.
Berry, Thomas, *Buddhism.* Hawthorn Books, 1967.
Dumoulin, Heinrich, S.J., *A History of Zen Buddhism.*★ Pantheon Books, 1963.
Reps, Paul, comp., *Zen Flesh, Zen Bones: A Collection of Zen and Pre-Zen Writings.*★ Doubleday Anchor Books, 1957.
Suzuki, Daisetz T.:
    An Introduction to Zen Buddhism.★ Black Cat, 1964.
    Zen and Japanese Culture. Pantheon Books, 1959.
    Zen Buddhism: Selected Writings of D. T. Suzuki. Ed. by William Barrett. Double-day Anchor Books, 1956.

ARTS AND ARCHITECTURE

Akiyama Terukazu, *Japanese Painting.* Skira, World Publishing, 1961.
Boger, H. Batterson, *The Traditional Arts of Japan.* Doubleday, 1964.
Drexler, Arthur, *The Architecture of Japan.* The Museum of Modern Art, 1955.
Engel, Heinrich, *The Japanese House, A Tradition for Contemporary Architecture.* Charles E. Tuttle, 1964.
Futagawa Yukio and Itoh Teiji, *The Essential Japanese House.* Tokyo, John Weather-hill, Bijutsu Shuppan-sha, joint publishers, 1967. (Distrib., Harper & Row.)
Iwamiya Takeji, *Katachi: Japanese Pattern and Design.* Harry N. Abrams, 1963.
Kidder, J. Edward, Jr.:
    Japanese Temples. Amsterdam, Harry N. Abrams, 1964.
    Masterpieces of Japanese Sculpture. Charles E. Tuttle, 1961.
Lee, Sherman E.:
    Japanese Decorative Style. Cleveland Museum of Art, 1961.
    History of Far Eastern Art. Harry N. Abrams, 1964.
Morse, Edward S., *Japanese Homes and Their Surroundings.*★ Dover Publications, 1961.

Munsterberg, Hugo:
    The Folk Arts of Japan. Charles E. Tuttle, 1958.
    Zen and Oriental Art. Charles E. Tuttle, 1965.
Newman, Alex R., and Egerton Ryerson, *Japanese Art, A Collector's Guide.* A. S. Barnes, 1965.
Noma Seiroku, *The Arts of Japan, Ancient and Medieval.* Transl. by John Rosenfield. Tokyo, Kodansha International, 1966. (U. S. Distrib., Japan Publications Trading Co., Rutland, Vt.)
Paine, Robert Treat and Alexander Soper, *The Art and Architecture of Japan.* Rev. ed. Penguin Books, 1960.
Tatsuo Shibato *et al.*, eds., *Japan, Art and Culture.* Tokyo, Government of Japan, 1964.
Yoshida Tetsuro, *The Japanese House and Garden.* Transl. from German by Marcus G. Sims. Frederick A. Praeger, 1957.

GENERAL CULTURAL STUDIES

Arai Hakuseki:
    The Armour Book in Honcho Gunkiko. Transl. by Y. Otsuka; rev. and ed. by H. Russell Robinson. Charles E. Tuttle, 1964.
    The Sword Book of Gunkiko. Transl. by H. L. Joly. Charles E. Tuttle, 1963.
Bush, Lewis, *Japanalia.* David McKay, 1959.
Ernst, Earle, *The Kabuki Theatre*★. Evergreen, 1959.
Halford, Aubrey S. and Giovanna M., *The Kabuki Handbook.* Charles E. Tuttle, 1965.
Japanese National Comm. for UNESCO, *Japan: Its Land, People, Culture.* Govern-ment of Japan Printing Bureau, 1958.
Joya, Mock, *Things Japanese.* 5th rev. ed., Tokyo, Tokyo News Service, 1964.
Keene, Donald, *No, The Classical Theatre of Japan.* Tokyo and Palo Alto, Kodansha International, 1966.
Morris, Ivan, *The World of the Shining Prince: Court Life in Ancient Japan.* Alfred A. Knopf, 1964.
Nakamura, Julia V., *The Japanese Tea Ceremony.* Peter Pauper Press, 1965.
Okakura Kakuzo, *The Book of Tea.*★ Dover, 1964.
Robinson, B. W., *The Arts of the Japanese Sword.* Faber & Faber, 1961.
Robinson, H. Russell, *Oriental Armour.* Walker, 1967.
Sadler, A. L., *Cha-no-yu, The Japanese Tea Ceremony.* Charles E. Tuttle, 1963.
Sakakibara Kozan, *The Manufacture of Armour and Helmets in 16th Century Japan.* Transl. by T. Wakameda. Rev. and ed. by H. Russell Robinson. Charles E. Tuttle, 1963.
Smith, Bradley, *Japan, A History in Art.* Simon and Schuster, 1964.
Smith, Cyril S., *History of Metallography.* University of Chicago Press, 1960.

TRANSLATIONS OF JAPANESE WORKS

Bownas, Geoffrey, and Anthony Thwaite, transls., *The Penguin Book of Japanese Verse.*† Penguin Books, 1964.
Chikamatsu Monzaemon, *Major Plays.* Transl. by Donald Keene. Columbia University Press, 1961.
Keene, Donald, *Anthology of Japanese Literature.*★ Evergreen, 1960.
McCullough, Helen Craig, transl., *The Taiheiki, A Chronicle of Medieval Japan.* Columbia University Press, 1959.
Murasaki, Lady, *The Tale of Genji.*★ Transl. by Arthur Waley. Modern Library, 1960.
Ryusaku Tsunoda, Wm. Theodore de Bary and Donald Keene, comps., *Sources of Japanese Tradition.*★ 2 vols. Columbia University Press, 1965.
Sadler, A. L., transl., *The Ten Foot Square Hut and Tales of the Heike.* Sydney, Angus & Robertson, 1928.
Sei Shonagon, *The Pillow Book.* Transl. by Arthur Waley. Allen & Unwin, 1957.

ACKNOWLEDGEMENT OF QUOTATIONS

Page 13: from *Sources of Japanese Tradition*, vol. 1, comp. by Ryusaku Tsunoda *et al.*, Columbia University Press, 1964, pp. 4–5. Pages 36–37, 37–38, 38: from *The Pillow Book of Sei Shonagon*, transl. by Arthur Waley, George Allen and Unwin, 1928, pp. 118–119, 126–127, 133–135. Page 39: from *The Tale of Genji*, by Lady Murasaki, transl. by Arthur Waley, The Modern Library, 1960, p. 79. Page 55: adapted from *A History of the Japanese People*, by Frank Brinkley, Encyclopaedia Britannica Corp., 1915, p. 255. Page 57: from *Japan, a Short Cultural History*, by G. B. Sansom, rev. ed., Appleton-Century-Crofts, 1962, p. 295. Page 58: from *Translations from Early Japanese Literature*, by Edwin O. Reischauer and Joseph K. Yamagiwa, Harvard University Press, 1964, p. 408. Pages 76–77: from *The Ten Foot Square Hut and Tales of the Heike*, transl. by A. L. Sadler, Angus & Robertson, 1928, pp. 54, 138, 154. Page 84: from *Zen and Japanese Culture*, by Daisetz T. Suzuki, Pantheon Books, 1959, p. 145. Page 101: from *The Onin War*, by H. Paul Varley, Columbia University Press, 1967, p. 141. Pages 116, 120, 120–121, 121 (col 1), 121 (col. 2, bottom), 121–122, 123, 140, 142–143: from *They Come to Japan*, ed. by Michael Cooper, S. J., University of California Press, 1965, pp. 6–7, 41–43, 45, 55–56, 94, 99, 103, 193, 201, 256–257. Pages 117, 118, 119, 121 (col. 2, top), 122, 122–123, 123–124, 139: from *The Christian Century in Japan*, by C. R. Boxer, University of California Press, 1967, pp. 37, 40, 51–55, 58, 138. Page 146: from G. B. Sansom, *op. cit.*, p. 410.

ART INFORMATION AND PICTURE CREDITS

The sources for the illustrations in this book are set forth below. Descriptive notes on the works of art are included. Credits for pictures positioned from left to right are separated by semicolons, from top to bottom by dashes. Photographers names which follow a descriptive note appear in parentheses. Abbreviations include "c." for century and "ca." for circa.

COVER—The samurai Kumagai Naozane, detail from six-part painted screen by Yusetsu Kaiho, 1650–1670, Sogoro Yabumoto, Osaka (T. Tanuma). 8–9—Map by Ed Young.

CHAPTER 1: 10—Sword guard with crab design, school of Owari openwork, iron, 16th c., Tokyo National Museum (Benrido). 12—*Haniwa* figures: head of a woman, from Yanagimoto, Tenri, Nara Pref., fired clay, Kofun Period, Matsubara Collection, Tokyo (M. Sakamoto); male dancer, from Konan, Saitama Pref., fired clay, 7th c., Tokyo National Museum (M. Sakamoto); monkey, from Tamatsukuri, Ibaragi Prefecture, fired clay, 7th c., Nakazawa Collection, Tokyo (M. Sakamoto). 17—Sketch of Gigaku dance mask, ink on wood, 7th c., Horyuji Temple, Nara (M. Sakamoto). 19—Geomancer's diagram, from Bruno Taut, *Houses and People of Japan*, Sanseido Co., Ltd., Tokyo, 1958. 21—Brian Brake from Rapho Guillumette. 22—Yoichi Midorikawa. 23—Brian Brake from Rapho Guillumette. 24—Norman Snyder. 25—Lynn Millar from Rapho Guillumette. 26–27—Brian Brake from Rapho Guillumette. 28–29—Hiroshi Hamaya.

CHAPTER 2: 30—Page of calligraphy, from the Collected Poems of Ise (*Ise-shu*), ink on ornamented paper, early 12th c., Philadelphia Museum of Art (Robert Crandall) 33—The guardian king Zochoten, Japanese cypress covered with dry lacquer and foil, 1124, Chusonji Temple, Hiraizumi, Iwate Pref. (Kazumi Yahagi). 37—Emperor's living quarters in Fujiwara mansion Higashi Sanjo-den, from the *Ruiju Zatsuyo-sho*, Kadokawa Publishing Co. 40—Muroji Temple plan, woodblock print, late Tokugawa period, Bijutsu-Shuppan, Tokyo. 43–53—Scenes from the illustrated scroll *Genji Monogatari* (*Tale of Genji*), attributed to Fujiwara Takayoshi, watercolour on rice paper, 12th c., Tokugawa Reimei-kai Foundation, Tokyo.

CHAPTER 3: 54—The samurai Taira Atsumori, detail from six-part painted screen by Yusetsu Kaiho, 1650–1670, Sogoro Yabumoto, Osaka (T. Tanuma). 56—Feudal estate of the Nakajo family, colour on paper, 1292, Nakajo Town Office, Niigata Pref. (Chuo Koronsha). 58—Portrait sculpture of Minamoto Yoritomo, polychromed wood, 13th c., Tokyo National Museum (Kodansha International). 63—Map by Rafael D. Palacios. 65–73—Illustrations from the *Tanki Yoryaku* (horseman's armour-wearing manual), by Masahiro Mura, printed on rice paper, 1837 rev. ed., The Metropolitan Museum of Art (Charles Phillips). 67—Detail of *Yoroi-hitatare* (armour robe), brocade, 14th c., Tokyo National Museum (T. Tanuma). 69—Detail of armour lacing and lamellae, made by Isagaru Miochin Ki Muneyuki, iron lamellae coated with lacquer and laced with green silk, ca. 1750, The Metropolitan Museum of Art (Paulus Leeser). 71—Helmet, made by Isagaru Miochin Ki Muneyuki, lacquered iron with gilded leather-lined turnbacks, ca.

1750, The Metropolitan Museum of Art (Paulus Leeser). 73—Armour sleeve, embossed iron over gilded and enamelled leather, black lacquered chain mail on brocaded cloth, 13th c., Kasuga Shrine, Nara (T. Tanuma).

CHAPTER 4: 74—Yakushi Buddha, bronze, 10th c., Horyuji Temple, Nara (Norman Snyder). 79—Tameshigiri (testing of sword blades) of the Yamada School, from Henri L. Joly and Inada Hogitaro, *The Sword and the Samé*, Charles E. Tuttle, New York, 1963. 82—Zen painting, by Sengai (1750–1837), Indian ink, Idemitsu Art Museum, Tokyo. 85—Fosco Maraini. 86—Yukio Futagawa. 87—Hiroshi Hamaya from Magnum. 88–89—Brian Brake from Rapho Guillumette. 90—Ken Domon. 91—Haruzo Ohaski—Ken Domon. 92–93—Brian Brake from Rapho Guillumette. 94–95—Haruzo Ohashi.

CHAPTER 5: 96—Waterfall scene, detail from six-part painted screen of the Four Seasons by Kano Motonobu, early 16th c., Freer Gallery of Art (Ray Schwartz). 99—Arrangement of *tatami* mats, from Edward S. Morse, *Japanese Homes and Their Surroundings*, Ticknor and Company, 1886. 102—Utensils of the tea ceremony, detail, satin brocade, 19th c., The Metropolitan Museum of Art. 107—Takeji Iwamiya. 108—Yukio Futagawa—Takeji Iwamiya. 109—Yukio Futagawa. 110—Yukio Futagawa—Takeji Iwamiya. 111—Yukio Futagawa—Takeji Iwamiya. 112—Takeji Iwamiya. 113—Takeji Iwamiya—Yukio Futagawa.

CHAPTER 6: 114—Rice-planting ceremony of *ta-ue*, detail from eight-part painted screen, late 16th c., Tokyo National Museum. 118—Portuguese carrack, detail from *Southern Barbarian Screen* (*Nambam-byoyu*) by Kano Naizen, colour on gold paper, early 17th c., Kobe Municipal Art Museum (T. Tanuma). 122–123—Carpentry drawings by Teiji Itoh, Institute of Japanese Architecture, Tokyo. 125–135—Scenes from the illustrated scroll *Sanjuniban Shokunin Uta-awase E-maki*, mineral paint on rice paper, 16th c., National Museum, Kyoto, courtesy of Shizuhiko Kosetsu, Osaka (T. Tanuma).

CHAPTER 7: 136—Portrait sketch of Toyotomi Hideyoshi, by Kano Sanraku, charcoal paint on strips of paper, late 16th c., Itsuo Art Museum, Osaka (T. Tanuma). 141—Portrait of Ryokei, ca. 1570, Stanford University Press. 142–143—Map by Rafael D. Palacios. 147–159—Munekazu Inoue.

CHAPTER 8: 160—Jesuit and Franciscan priests, detail from *Southern Barbarian Screen* (*Nambam-byoyu*) by Kano Naizen, colour on gold paper, early 17th c., Kobe Municipal Art Museum (T. Tanuma). 163—Hideyoshi fan, Indian ink, gold and red colour on paper, late 16th c., Kinta Muto (Chuokoronsha). 166—Kosaku Ito. 169–181—Norman Snyder.

ACKNOWLEDGEMENTS

For help given in the preparation of this book, the editors are particularly indebted to Marius B. Jansen, Professor, Department of History, Princeton University, Princeton, New Jersey. The editors are also grateful to Shujiro Shimada, Professor, Department of Art and Archaeology, Princeton University; Carl Sesar, Instructor, Department of Asian Languages and Literature, Wesleyan University, Middletown, Connecticut; John Max Rosenfield, Associate Professor of Fine Arts, Fogg Art Museum, Harvard University, Cambridge, Massachusetts; Walter W. Ristow, Associate Chief, Geography and Map Division, and Andrew Y. Kuroda, Orientalia Division, The Library of Congress, Washington, D. C.; Soshin S. Hayasaki, Tea Ceremony Society of Urasenke, New York City; Gordon Washburn, Director, Asia House Gallery, New York City; Cyril S. Smith, Professor, Metallurgy and Materials Science Department, Massachusetts Institute of Technology, Cambridge, Massachusetts; J. Randolph Castile, Educational Director, Japan Society, New York City; Harold P. Stern, Assistant Director, and Ray Schwartz, Freer Gallery of Art, Smithsonian Institution, Washington, D. C.; Helmut Nickel, Curator, Arms and Armor, The Metropolitan Museum of Art, New York City; Ludwig Glaezer, Associate Curator, Architecture and Design, The Museum of Modern Art, New York City; Reiko Uyeshima and Hirotake Suzuki, New York City; Ken Harada, Grand Master of Ceremonies, Toshio Tsuji and Sueyoshi Abe, Board of Ceremonies, Imperial Household, Tokyo; Nagatake Asano, Director, Jo Okada, Chief Curator, Hisatoyo Ishida, Head of Research, Kiyoshi Imanaga, Sadao Kicuchi, and Junji Nakajima, Tyoko National Museum; Kairchiro Nezu, Director, and Hisaw Sugahara, Associate Director, Nezu Art Museum, Tokyo; Yoshinobu Tokugawa, Director, and Masana Kamimura, Assistant, Tokugawa Reimeikai Foundation, Tokyo; J. Edward Kidder Jr., Professor of Art and Archeology, International Christian University, Tokyo; Kanichiro Kubota, Director, Kokusai Bunka Shinkokai, Tokyo: Kyotaro Nishikawa, Curator, National Commission for Protection of Cultural Properties, Tokyo; Atsushi Oshita, Editor in Chief, Bijutsu

Shuppan-Sha, Tokyo; Yoshitomo Okamoto, Tokyo; Father Gino K. Piovesana, S.J., Director of the Board of Regents, Takanao Nakada, Dean, and Father Masao Tsuchida, S.J., Department of Japanese Literature, Father Fernando G. Gutierrez, S.J., Assistant Professor of Art History, and Father Arcadio Schwade, S.J., Assistant Professor of History, Sophia University, Tokyo; Ruy G. de Brito E Cunha, Second Secretary, Portuguese Embassy, Tokyo; Teiji Itoh, Institute of Japanese Architecture, Tokyo; Keizo Saji, Director, Suntory Museum of Art, Tokyo; Shinkichi Osaki, Curator, and Nobuo Shibata, Deputy Curator, Okura Shuko-Kan Museum, Tokyo; Kanamaro Kaneko, Chuo Koron, Tokyo; Sazo Idemitsu, Director, Idemitsu Art Museum, Tokyo; Ataru Kobayashi, Tokyo; Charels E. Tuttle, Tokyo; Kikutaro Saito, Tokyo; Hiroshi Doi, Director, Executive Offices, Shosoin, Nara; Osamu Kurata, Director, and Shoichi Uehara, Curator, Nara National Museum, Nara; Saneharu Sanjo, Chief Priest, and Suketada Chidori, Priest, Kasuga Shrine, Nara; Zenryu Tsukamoto, Director, Jiro Umezu, Chief of Research, and Motoo Yoshimura, Curator of Applied Arts, Kyoto National Museum, Kyoto; Ruth Fuller Sasaki, Ryosen-An, Daitokuji, Kyoto; Soshitsu Sen, Tea Master, and Soshin S. Hayasaki, Ura-Senke, Kyoto; Y. Ernest Satow, Kyoto; Kazuo Shibata, General Affairs Section, Shiga Prefecture Government; Shizuo Sudo, Director, and Shoun Ishimrau, Biwa-Ko Bunkakan, Otsu; Ryoichi Okamoto, Director, and Shingo Akiyama, Researcher, Osaka Castle, Osaka; Yoshiro Kitamura, Director, Namban Culture Center, Osaka; Goroku Kumazawa, Director, Tokugawa Art Museum, Nagoya; Yasuo Orimo, Director, Kobe Municipal Art Museum of Namban; Rihei Okada, Director, and Kokichi Ono, Curator, Itsuo Art Museum; Ryoichi Murata, Director, Kanagawa Prefectural Museum, Yokohama; Nishikawa Takeshi, Director of Administration, Himeji Castle, Himeji; Marguerite Deneck, Assistant Curator, Musée Guimet, Paris; Roger Goepper, Museum für Ostasiatische Kunst, Cologne; B. W. Robinson, Victoria and Albert Museum, London.

INDEX

W

Wa (early south-western Japan), Chinese reports of, 13
Wako (pirates), 105–106, 116
War tales, Kamakura, 76–77
Warfare: castle defence, 148, 150, 155, 157; early feudal age, 55–56, 76–77; late Heian Age, 41–42, 55; love of, 11, 12; Minamoto v. Taira, 58–59; Muromachi period, 100, 103, 105, 118–119; of Nobunaga, 137–141; samurai, 57, 65–73; samurai man-to-man tactics, 62, 105, 138; tactics of Age of the Country at War, 105, 138, 139, 140–141
Warrior class, 55, 57, 60, 76–79; and Zen Buddhism, 83–84. See also

Samurai
Weapons, *10, 77; fire-arms, 106, 138–139, 140–141, 168; of foot-soldiers, 105, 138–139; of samurai, *54, 57, *65, 77–79; swords, 70, 77–79
White Heron castle, at Himeji, *147–159
Winding water banquets, 36
Women, 116; early standing of, 13; of Heian aristocracy, 36–38; as Kamakura warriors, 77; poets of Heian Age, 34, 36–39; as rulers, 13; subordination of, 13, 104
Working class, *126–135
World War II, 63–64, 77, 82
Writing: Japanese syllabic, 34; use of Chinese system, 15, 33, 34. See also

Calligraphy

X

Xavier, Francis, 116–117, 118, 120

Y

Yamato Court, 14–15
Yamato plain, 14, 19
Yayoi culture, 13
Yellow Sea, map 8
Yodo river, 31, map 63
Yoritomo. See Minamoto family

Yoshiaki. See Ashikaga family
Yoshimasa. See Ashikaga family
Yoshimitsu. See Ashikaga family

Z

Zazen (meditation), 83
Zen Buddhism, 82–84, 98; aesthetics of, 84, 86, 101, 107; gardens, 84, *85–89, *92–93, 94; and ink painting, 86; origin of tea ceremony in, 101; secular activities of clergy, 98, 99; temples and monasteries, 84, 98; and violence by sword, 84; Zen drawing, *82
Zori (slippers), *112

xxxxx

Typesetting by Alfred Utesch, Hamburg
Smeets Lithographers, Weert, Printed in Holland
Bound by Proost and Brandt N.V., Amsterdam